Harry

The Unauthorized Biography

T0017829

Harry

The Unauthorized Biography

DANNY WHITE

Michael O'Mara Books Limited

This revised paperback edition first published in 2023

First published in Great Britain in 2021 by
Michael O'Mara Books Limited
9 Lion Yard
Tremadoc Road
London SW4 7NQ

A CIP catalogue record for this book is available from the British Library.

Papers used by Michael O'Mara Books Limited are natural, recyclable
products made from wood grown in sustainable forests. The manufacturing
processes conform to the environmental regulations of the country of
origin.

ISBN: 978-1-78929-513-9 in paperback print format
ISBN: 978-1-78929-263-3 in ebook format

1 2 3 4 5 6 7 8 9 10
Cover design by Natasha Le Coultre
Designed and typeset by Claire Cater
Front cover image: Ron Smits / London Entertainment / Shutterstock
Back cover image: Kevin Mazur / Getty Images
Printed and bound by CPI Group (UK) Ltd, Croydon, CR0 4YY
www.mombooks.com

CONTENTS

INTRODUCTION

Just like his musical heroes, Harry Styles rewrites the rules. When a successful boy band splits, its former members can either live off the glory of their previous heights, disappear altogether or crumble emotionally, occasionally being snapped by paparazzi, eating junk food and looking sad.

Harry Styles did not go in any of these directions. Since One Direction went on hiatus in 2016 he has, instead, gone about becoming the king of the world. He has had three consecutive number-one albums on the *Billboard* 200 and ascended to number four on the *Billboard* Hot 100 with his debut solo single, 2017's 'Sign of the Times'. Rather than banging on with the stadium pop of his old band, he has instead artistically reinvented himself, and borrowed elements from grander, more distant acts, like David Bowie, Fleetwood Mac and Mick Jagger.

Harry may turn out to be the most successful solo star to emerge from a boy band – ever. Although Robbie Williams has enjoyed colossal success and fortune, there has never been the sense that he has ever tried to truly reinvent himself. The only other former boy band star to have so successfully reinvented himself is Justin Timberlake, who went from teen boy band NSYNC to an adult R&B star who people of any age, gender or sexuality were happy to openly appreciate. You wouldn't bet against Harry eclipsing Timberlake.

Harry has the confidence and stature to disappear for months on end but, when he returns, it is with just as much momentum as when he left. He doesn't waste time, energy and dignity by trying to be in the public eye every minute of every day. It all smacks of a drive for longevity and a love of authenticity, rather than a desperate scramble for what he can get before people forget about One Direction and *The X Factor*. In fact, you get the feeling he'd be quite happy for people to forget about One Direction and *The X Factor* altogether.

A word that frequently comes up when people comment on his music, his live performances and his interactions with other people is not one you often hear used about former boy band members: subtlety. He is a refined character with poise and natural star quality. *The X Factor* made Liam Payne, Louis Tomlinson, Niall Horan and Zayn Malik into stars. But Harry? He already was a star; One Direction just made it official.

Yet there remains a lot of mystery around the man. His lack of neediness and casual self-confidence means he has not felt the need to perform soul-baring gimmicks to grab momentary media attention. It is only in his music that one can sometimes tap into a vulnerable, personal place into which he rarely lets his fans. This makes telling the story of his life all the more satisfying and the details more revealing.

With his renowned part in the film *Dunkirk*, he has also become an actor. Yet, whichever parts Harry goes on to play on the big screen, the most magnificent part he will ever play is that of Harry Styles. As we will see, it is a complex, demanding role – but a fun one. Harry Styles is a solo singer born out of the most poppy of reality television, now alluding to the credible likes of Pink Floyd and Bowie in his material.

But Harry Styles is also a clothes horse who wins best-dressed gongs and absolutely shines in Gucci. He is a pin-up for all ages from teenagers to grandparents. Harry Styles is also a 'woke' young man, speaking out against racism and animal abuse, and a superhero, fighting toxic masculinity. He is an androgynous figure and LGBT ally who tells his fans they can be whatever they wish to be.

Anyone who can nail all of that has something beyond star quality. Pop managers and celebrity handlers cannot teach what Harry Styles has, or they'd be doing it with all their clients. The roots of Harry's stardom go much deeper and began to grow long before he set foot on the famous *X Factor* audition stage. Stars like him do not come along very often and it's a treat to be alive as one of them reaches their peak. In an article of praise for *GQ* magazine, Daphne Bugler argued that 'the world doesn't deserve Harry Styles'. Yet the world does have Harry Styles. Here's his journey.

CHAPTER ONE

A STAR IS BORN

When he looks back over his childhood, Harry remembers a whole lot of happiness. 'I had a really nice upbringing, I feel very lucky,' he said. 'I had a great family and always felt loved.' So don't expect him to follow the well-trodden path of pop stars speaking and singing about demons left over from a torturous childhood. He won't pretend that things were worse than they were. 'There's nothing worse than an inauthentic tortured person,' he said.

His childhood was actually one of adoring family support. He said: 'Our house was always filled with loving each other.' No one gave him more love than his mother, Anne. 'At the end of the day, he's my little baby,' said Anne of Harry. However famous, rich or old her son gets, she'll always remember him as the baby she brought into the world, all those years ago. Harry was born on 1 February 1994. It was a Tuesday when he was delivered at the Alexandra Hospital in Redditch, Worcestershire. It had been a hurried arrival at the hospital – 'We only just made it in time,' remembered his father, Des.

Harry was Anne's second child – she already had a young daughter called Gemma, who Harry has said is the 'smart one' in the family. Anne named her precious baby son Harry Edward. Legend has it that she chose his first name following an incident during her pregnancy. According to a retired ambulance worker who helped her when she fell ill at a concert in Birmingham, when Anne spotted his name badge, she said: 'You're quite nice. If it's a boy, I'm going to call him Harry.'

His name and birth were registered at Bromsgrove Registration Office a few days after he was born. If you believe in astrology the date of his birth makes Harry an Aquarian. Those who fall under this star sign are free-spirited and unconventional. Those who follow astrology say you can always spot an Aquarian by their wacky fashion style, curious pastimes and rebellious attitudes. Harry's sense of style is certainly out there and he has bucked what is expected of stars of his origins.

As the youngest in his family, Harry is said to be likely to have certain traits, according to the 'birth order' theory, which supposes that a person's behaviour is determined by whether they are the first, middle, youngest or only child. For instance, the theory argues that youngest children tend to be the most free-spirited because their parents become increasingly laid-back in their attitude towards parenting from the second child onwards.

So both the star sign he was born under and the familial sequence he was born in suggest Harry should be a free spirit, and it is true that his spirit is more liberated than most. Other qualities attributed to youngest siblings include them being fun-loving, attention-seeking and outgoing. Free-spirited last-borns are believed to be more open to unconventional experiences. As we will see, much of this rings true with Harry.

In fact, a lot of the signs of his path in life were there from the start and perhaps determined by the circumstances of his birth.

'He's always loved attention and making people laugh,' Anne told *NOW* magazine of her beloved son. 'He's certainly not shy about himself. Ever since he was young he's made people smile. I always thought he'd end up on the stage.'

But first, there was a lot of growing up to be done. Harry's most formative years were spent in Cheshire, in the north-west of England. Cheshire is an area of lush rural splendour surrounding a number of villages and towns. When he auditioned for *The X Factor*, Harry described the area as 'quite boring – nothing much happens there', though on a more positive note he admitted, with that winning cheeky smile we all now know so well, that it is 'picturesque'.

Holmes Chapel, one of those villages, is where Harry spent much of his childhood. Cheshire itself is not an area with a particularly famous artistic heritage, though it is the home area of rock singers Ian Curtis and Tim Burgess. However, thanks to his fame, Harry is now one of Cheshire's most celebrated sons. He has well and truly put the place on the map.

Before he went to school, he was sent to a nursery called Happy Days. It seems a well-named institution as Harry did indeed spend many enjoyable times there. It was a small establishment, so he was never short of attention and care. Indeed, one of the staff members had previously babysat Harry, so Happy Days seemed almost like a home from home for him. Among his activities there was to draw on slices of bread using food colouring and then toast it. 'They were happy days to be fair,' he said in One Direction's official book, *Dare to Dream*.

Once he gets into his stride, Harry is rarely short of a word. He was just the same as a chatty toddler. Ever since he spoke his first word, Harry always had plenty to say. His first word was 'cat' – Anne will probably always remember how, one day, he pointed at her parents' black cat and said: 'Cat!' He loved animals as a kid. So much so that he shared his dummy with the family dog, Max, who was a Border Collie mix.

During his nursery years he was a well-behaved boy and concentrated on playing with toys and participating in games. For as long as anyone can remember, he has always been a fun-loving chap. Harry was always encouraged to express himself, which is such a key factor in the development of any budding artist. Not for him a childhood of discouragement and uninterest, which can crush the development of would-be singers. Instead, his more artistic and expressive characteristics were nurtured and encouraged both at home and at the nursery.

He had many such tendencies: Harry learned to juggle and also tried his hand at some musical instruments. He was becoming something of an all-rounder, as he was a humorous and entertaining little boy as well. Even back then, Harry was proving to be the walking embodiment of a variety show. He could have entered his future mentor's other series, *Britain's Got Talent*, across several disciplines.

'I wasn't one of those boys who thought girls were smelly and didn't like them; I was kind of friends with everyone.'

Later, he was sent to the Hermitage Primary School, where he wore grey trousers, a white polo shirt and a navy jumper. He particularly enjoyed English and RE classes. In English he found he was good at expressing himself on the page and often got good grades for his essays. He could be cheeky, for sure, but rather than ever truly misbehaving – he only got in one fight throughout his school years – he channelled his drive into hard work.

Many of his fellow pupils remember him fondly. He was a friendly and outgoing pupil who enjoyed the company of girls as well as boys. 'I wasn't one of those boys who thought girls were smelly and didn't like them; I was kind of friends with everyone,' he remembered in the official 1D book. He has also described himself as 'such a mummy's boy'. This strong relationship with women from a young age helped shape him into the personality he is today. As we shall see, he credits the prominence of women in his childhood for many good things.

But it was performance that got his young blood pumping most. With his extrovert side growing nearly as fast as his body did, he really looked forward to drama classes. Through these classes, he made his first ever public singing appearance. 'The first time I sang properly was in a school production – the rush that I got was something that I really enjoyed and wanted to do more of,' he said. That rush was the feeling of his love of performing and being in the spotlight being satisfied. He had found himself.

'The first time I sang properly was in a school production – the rush that I got was something that I really enjoyed and wanted to do more of.'

However, as many creatives and performers have found, having that desire fulfilled for the first time does not satisfy it. Far from it – it actually pours fuel over it, turning it into a fire that must be sated by further appearances. No sooner had one performance ended than he was ready for the next one. He would give impromptu performances in the school car park. As parents arrived to collect their children, they would sometimes find Harry standing up on the back seat of his parents' car, and singing through the open car window.

The plays that he appeared in included *Chitty Chitty Bang Bang*, in which Harry played the part of Buzz Lightyear. This being a school production, some liberties had been taken with tradition … As an Aquarian by star sign, Harry has always been comfortable with experimentation, so that was fine by him. On another occasion he played the title role in a play about a mouse called Barney: he absolutely nailed it as Barney the Mouse, wearing his big sister

Gemma's tights and big glued-on ears. 'I like to think I was a good mouse,' he said in the One Direction official book.

Another time he appeared as the Elvis-like Pharaoh in the school's production of *Joseph and the Amazing Technicolor Dreamcoat*. It is a perfect part for Harry: Pharaoh appears as a comedic and charismatic turn in the second half of the play, upping the ante and enthralling everyone. He was brilliant and for this he got his first written review. The school newsletter said: 'We all remember Harry for a fantastic performance.' Gemma remembers: 'Even then he had that sort of magnetism that made people just want to watch him. He made people laugh.'

He was also a sporty kid. He played in goal for his local football team, Holmes Chapel Hurricanes, and also enjoyed badminton and cricket. He credits his father with his flair for badminton, as Des, too, was a fine player. Harry enjoyed the skill involved in badminton and was happy to take part in a less popular sport. He enjoyed making new friends through playing, including those from other schools.

* * *

However, despite his happy description of his childhood, when he was seven Harry's life, which had been generally very happy and enjoyable until then, took a more challenging turn. His parents took him and Gemma to one side and explained to them that they were going to get divorced. Poor Harry – his first reaction was to burst into tears. It was so upsetting to have this bombshell dropped on him.

He loved both his mum and dad so he couldn't bear the thought of them going their separate ways and the family being broken up. At seven years of age Harry would most likely have been in a double bind: old enough to understand the pain caused by the separation but not yet mature enough to really take it on board or to control his own reaction to the pain. Children of his age who face such a testing upheaval can go through feelings of grief, shame, resentment, confusion and even anger as they come to terms with the situation.

Later, Des recalled the moment that he told Harry and Gemma the news, describing it as 'the worst day of my life'. Speaking to the *Daily Record*, he said: 'He was only about seven when I sat them down and told them I was leaving. Everybody was in tears.' The memories are so vivid and painful. 'We were sitting in the lounge. Gemma and Harry were sitting on the floor in front of us, Anne and I on the sofa, and both of them were crying. Generally, you wouldn't see him cry as much as maybe some kids do – he wasn't generally emotional or a cry baby – but he cried then.'

Des added that he 'didn't just leave – it was a decision we should split. Things weren't good for a while and it was the best way forward.' Indeed, Des remained in the family home for some time, sleeping in the spare room, to create a sense of evolution rather than an abrupt exit.

After he did formally leave, Des found he suffered from his own struggles and began to recall Harry's earliest days. 'Of course, I missed Harry and Gemma, as you would unless you were some sort of monster,' he said. What had been his life as a father suddenly changed, almost beyond recognition. 'It was tough. I used to feed him every night at half ten, change his nappy, put him to bed when he was a baby and then I was no longer living with them.'

Although he gives most credit to Anne for how she brought up Harry after he left, he still had an impact on Harry's life. 'He's polite and well mannered, he's trained up properly, but it wasn't me, of course not, it would be Anne. But in his younger years, it was me. I say show me the lad at seven and I'll show you the man, so I was there then.' Although Des left the family home when Harry was a child, they still have a strong bond now, so the divorce didn't cause long-lasting damage.

As for Harry, he remembers the time of the separation as a 'weird time' and says he did cry about what was going on. He says he 'didn't really get what was going on properly'. However, he still felt 'loved and supported' by both parents throughout. 'Honestly, when you're that young you can kind of block it out,' he said.

After the break-up was confirmed, Anne and the kids moved deeper into the Cheshire countryside. Their new home was above a pub. Harry made a new friend, a boy called Reg. Although Reg was a little older than Harry, the two hit it off and were soon inseparable. In the summer, they would cycle the two miles to Great Budworth Ice Cream Farm, near Budworth Heath. Harry vividly remembers these trips for a treat and has since been back; on its Facebook page, the outlet posted a photo of an all-grown-up Harry with two members of staff, and the caption: 'I scream, you scream, we all scream for … Harry Styles!'

Another part of Harry's life that Des was responsible for was first getting his son interested in the art form that would catapult him to global fame and fortune: music.

Among the musicians Des introduced Harry to was the King of Rock'n'Roll himself – Elvis Presley. The singer of a string of hits including 'Heartbreak Hotel', 'Can't Help Falling in Love', 'Hound Dog' and 'Blue Suede Shoes' was a firm favourite of the family. As it became clear that Harry loved to sing, his grandfather bought him a karaoke machine as a present. The first songs that Harry crooned along to on it were by Elvis Presley, including the yearning lyrics of 'The Girl of My Best Friend'. His songs echoed around the house and family members would find themselves dancing around and singing along. 'Elvis was such an icon for me growing up,' Harry told *The Face*. 'There was something almost sacred about him, almost like I didn't want to touch him.'

Harry also remembers hearing more sophisticated music as a kid. For instance, *The Dark Side of the Moon* by Pink Floyd was played by his parents. 'I couldn't really get it,' he says. But he does remember thinking: 'This is really f**king cool.' The influence of the 1970s prog-rockers would later be felt keenly in his solo music and it was in the family home during his childhood that the seeds were sown.

Des also remembers that Harry's effect on the opposite sex started before he was famous – long before he was famous. 'We went on holiday once to Cyprus when he was nine and as we left there was a whole melee of teenage girls, sixteen-, seventeen-year-olds gathered by the side of the bus saying, "Bye Harry, we love you."' How did he do that?' he said. Long before he even auditioned for *The X Factor*, Harry had the voice and the way with girls that would win hearts. Harry's friend Will Sweeny also noted the future star's naturally charming way with women. He told the *Daily Star*: 'I've known him since he was four years old. I know it sounds funny, but even in primary school he had a few girls on the go. From year four, when he was about ten, Harry started with proper girlfriends. He just had this unbelievable way with girls all his life.'

'I like someone I can have a conversation with, and I would always look for someone who could get on with my parents.'

However, while he could charm the opposite sex there is no suggestion that he was anything less than respectful. Later, in a separate interview with *Sugarscape*, Sweeny said that Harry's girlfriends were 'long-term'. He adds: 'He was dead caring to them, too; he'd never cheat or mess them around. He talked about how a girl seemed like a nice person, not what her body was like. It's what's inside the person that matters to Harry.'

In One Direction's official book, Harry said he 'doesn't have a type' and adds that though he may not find a girl attractive immediately, he can sometimes change how he feels because their personality begins to attract him. 'I like someone I can have a conversation with, and I would always look for someone who could get on with my parents,' he wrote.

Later, he remarked that he likes girls who play hard to get. 'The fun part is the chase, so if you speak to me, play a bit hard to get,' he told *Top of the Pops* magazine. 'I think it's attractive when someone turns you down. You don't want someone to say yes straight away, do you?' Perhaps this statement was, at least in part, an attempt to get his millions of screaming female fans to calm down a bit.

Nevertheless, he had that magical quality that many do, indeed, describe as the 'X Factor'. Right back into his childhood, it was rearing its enchanting head. 'He's just got this fantastic personable demeanour to him. Clearly he's a bit special,' said Des. 'It's not just his looks but he's very charming, it's like a gift really. I always knew he'd succeed at whatever he did because he'd always charm people, from performing in the car or on holiday he'd always be able to hold a crowd or hold a room even when he was a kid.'

Indeed, it was when he was at the Holmes Chapel Comprehensive school on Selkirk Drive in Cheshire that Harry stumbled upon an exciting way of further fulfilling his desire to perform in front of an audience. He was invited to join a rock band. A friend of his, named Will, was looking for a lead vocalist for a band he was assembling. He asked Harry to come along and practise with the band. All the members were very happy with handsome Harry as their frontman and the band's line-up was complete.

Then they just needed to agree on a name for themselves. It was Harry who suggested the random name White Eskimo. It is a rather strange moniker – it sounds more like a nightclub or a cocktail than a teenage rock band. One could even imagine a horse with that name competing in the Grand National. Nevertheless it was certainly distinctive and nobody had any better ideas, so they went with it. Harry has an inventive mind: this would not be the last time that he came up with a band name.

The band were influenced by punk-pop acts such as Californian band Blink-182. Harry is also a fan of Jack's Mannequin and other related artists. However, three of his biggest musical inspirations stood entirely outside the punk-pop genre during their iconic careers: Michael Jackson, Elvis Presley and Freddie Mercury. Other songs he loved during his childhood include 'Free Fallin'' by John Mayer and he also had a soft spot for the material of Michael Bublé. Each member of White Eskimo had their own influences – together they made for a fairly decent musical outfit.

Soon, they were playing at school events and a wedding. The first song that White Eskimo ever performed live together was Bryan Adams' 'Summer of '69'. Then the band noticed there was a local talent show being held for groups. They decided to enter it, as Harry later explained to *X Factor* host Dermot O'Leary on the programme. 'We entered a Battle of the Bands competition about a year and a half ago and we won. Winning Battle of the Bands and playing in front of that many people really showed me that's what I wanted to do. I got such a thrill when I was in front of people singing, it made me want to do more and more.'

The victory had also made an impression on Harry's head teacher Denis Oliver, who was present at the competition that was held at the school canteen. Mr Oliver remembered later: 'White Eskimo won Battle of the Bands here when he was in Year Ten. He's performed in a lot of assemblies.' Harry's singing had clearly made quite an impact on those who populated his first live audiences.

Some of the children who were at those shows have since remembered what they saw. Bethany Lysycia, for instance, told the *Crewe Chronicle*: 'They were really good. Everyone was really impressed, especially with Harry. We all knew he could sing because we would see him singing in the corridors all the time. He was always going to be a star and I think he's getting better and better.'

Videos have been published on the internet of the band performing at a wedding. Again, the band are performing 'Summer of '69'. Although Harry's voice is, naturally, quite a lot higher in these videos than it is now, he cuts a familiar figure on the stage: he bounces, looks down at the floor as he takes deep breaths, and generally comes across as the same lad who went on to join One Direction. Another song that they played regularly was 'Are You Gonna Be My Girl' by the band Jet. In another video the band is seen rehearsing. Their sense of fun is clear.

'We wrote a couple of songs,' said Harry. 'One was called "Gone In A Week". It was about luggage. "I'll be gone in a week or two/ Trying to find myself someplace new/I don't need any jackets or shoes/The only luggage I need is you."' Not the sort of songwriting that would trouble the judges of the Ivor Novello awards but decent enough patter for lads of their age at the time.

> He was becoming a local celebrity and pin-up long before he became nationally and then internationally famous.

Their wedding performance had even earned them their first pay packet. The band was paid £160 for the show which they split evenly between them. As he remembered fondly, they were also offered free sandwiches. However, more valuable than the money and sarnies combined was the experience and the feedback. People were telling him that he was a natural singer and frontman. His charisma and stage presence were such that one guest at the wedding, a music producer and therefore a man with expert eyes, compared him with one of British music history's finest frontmen, Mick Jagger of the Rolling Stones.

What an honour: Harry felt so proud and excited by all the positive feedback he received. He was becoming a local celebrity and pin-up long before he became nationally and then internationally famous. That fact, together with his boyish good looks and charming ways, meant he was getting even more attention from girls long before he shot to national fame through *The X Factor*. He rates a female friend he had at the age of six as his first close female friend. She was the daughter of a friend of Anne's and the two were very sweet together. Harry even bought them matching teddy bears. He describes her as 'the cutest little girl'. At the age of twelve he got his first proper girlfriend and he has stated that his 'first snog' was with a girl from his school.

A girl called Lydia Cole told the *Crewe Chronicle* that Harry had been her first boyfriend, while they were both at school. 'What you see on screen is what you get,' she said. 'That's Harry – he's always been charming and cheeky.' Rumours that circulated about Harry once he became famous through One Direction portray him as very experienced with girls and very quick to show off about his prowess. 'Harry was bragging about how many girls he'd slept with,' an 'insider' quoted by *Now* magazine claimed. 'The number he said was six.' They added: 'Harry's very flirty.' Of all the band members it was Harry who seemed most assured when dealing with attractive female personalities during their time on *The X Factor* and beyond. The legacy of his past experience was visible in the smooth, confident and assured persona he took when speaking with them, which belied his tender years.

He remembers that his first girlfriend was called Abigail. 'My first proper girlfriend used to have one of those laughs. There was also a little bit of mystery with her because she didn't go to our school. I just worshipped the ground she walked on. And she knew probably to a fault, a little. That was a tough one. I was fifteen. She used to live an hour and a half away on the train, and I worked in a bakery … I'd finish on Saturdays at 4.30 and it was a 4.42 train and if I missed it there wasn't one for another hour or two.

'So, I'd finish and sprint to the train station. Spent seventy per cent of my wages on train tickets. Later, I'd remember her perfume. Little things. I smell that perfume all the time. I'll be in a lift or a reception and say to someone, "Alien, right?" And sometimes they're impressed and sometimes they're a little creeped out. "Stop smelling me.'"

As for his family, it got a new member when his mother met his stepdad Robin. The couple had been careful to consider Harry and Gemma's feelings by introducing their partnership gradually and sensitively. Harry thought Robin was great and was delighted – if a bit amused – to learn that he had proposed to Anne while they sat watching the soap opera *Coronation Street*.

However, his need to earn cash was always a preoccupation for him. He loved having a few quid in his pocket, so he took a job working at a local business, the W. Mandeville Bakery. His boss, Simon Wakefield, told the BBC that Harry had been a model employee. 'He used to clean the floor at night and work on a Saturday, serving customers in the shop. He was great, he was good to have around – there was always a good atmosphere when he was about.' Harry's former boss said the youngster 'was really popular with the customers when he used to work on the counter'. One can imagine his charisma and boyish good looks going down a treat with customers. Looking back at it later, he was enthusiastic but low-key about that part of his childhood. 'I worked for the old ladies,' he remembered. 'Very nice old ladies.'

For his longer-term job plans, one ambition he had at school was to work as a physiotherapist. 'We had a workshop at school where we went in to talk about what we wanted to do and essentially someone told me there were no jobs in that, so I should pick something else. I was a little stumped, to be honest.' He also dreamed of studying law and going on to work in that sector. 'So I decided I wanted to be a lawyer. This happened before I had to start working hard enough to be a lawyer. Now I can be like, I would have been a lawyer,' he said. However, he has admitted that he might have found it too hard. He is perhaps being harsh on himself there, because his GCSE results show that Harry was a bright and promising student – he got 12 A* to C grades.

Meanwhile, his true ambition continued to bubble up inside

him. He wanted to take his flair for music and his experiences with White Eskimo to a whole new level. Having watched *The X Factor* growing up and with his fledgling success with the band, this seemed like a route worth trying.

So he grabbed an application form, which Anne filled in for him and then posted off. Harry's mum was playing her supportive part as ever. While he counted down the days to his audition, he told his White Eskimo bandmates what he planned to do and they said they had no hard feelings over this. The bass guitarist Nick Clough said: 'We're happy for him and wish him all the best.' The lead guitarist, Haydn Morris, said: 'Everyone here at school is behind him. It's great.'

Meanwhile, his true ambition continued to bubble up inside him. He wanted to take his flair for music and his experiences with White Eskimo to a whole new level.

Harry was ready for some more excitement. Although he remembers a loving childhood, he has also spoken of it feeling a little dour at times. The areas he lived in were quiet and at school, he said, he was 'not really interested' in what was going on. He wanted more thrills and he was about to get much, much more than that.

CHAPTER TWO

TIME TO
FACE THE MUSIC

A nne was not and is not the archetypal pushy mum. We have seen how some parents actively discourage their children's creative potential, stamping out the dreams of their offspring. Julia Cameron has written compellingly of this harmful trend in her seminal book, *The Artist's Way*. However, the other extreme of the spectrum can also be damaging. Often, stories of successful singers – particularly those who found fame at a young age – include the ominous and frankly abusive presence of an ambitious and bossy parent, who almost bullies their child onto the stage. While this approach can produce results in the short term, in the long run it often leads to mental health issues for the people who were pushed under the spotlight. Michael Jackson said that his father Joseph would be physically abusive of him and his siblings as they rehearsed as a band. Jackson told Oprah: 'If you didn't do it the right way, he would tear you up, really get you.'

There needs to be encouragement but not too much. Getting it right is tricky but Anne managed it: she was supportive but not pushy – a really good balance. 'She's never made me feel like I have to prove myself,' Harry said of her. However, this is not to say that she did not encourage Harry in his dream of auditioning on *The X Factor*. 'I've always wanted to do it and my mum's always wanted me to do it,' he said when he was asked why he had decided to audition.

> He had been told by lots of people that he had potential but Harry was grounded and self-aware enough to take praise from loved ones with a pinch of salt.

He had been told by lots of people that he had potential but Harry was grounded and self-aware enough to take praise from loved ones with a pinch of salt. 'When I get told I'm good, it's by my friends or my family,' he said. 'So I want to find out from someone who, like, knows what they're talking about – to see if they're lying or not.'

Harry auditioned in Manchester. Although he had sung onstage in front of audiences with White Eskimo, this experience was on a whole new scale: a 3,000-strong live audience, television cameras and the unforgiving presence of the notorious *X Factor* judges. Very different. But he could count on plenty of support in the form of an entourage of family and friends. Each member of which wore T-shirts bearing the slogan: 'We think Harry has the *X Factor*!' The men wore black T-shirts, the women sported white ones. It made for a striking image as well as a bit of fun. As for Harry, he was wearing a low-slung white T-shirt with a loose grey cardigan and a green patterned scarf. That ability to wear stylish outfits with insouciance was already there.

* * *

Before taking to the stage itself, it was time for him to speak to the presenter, Dermot O'Leary. 'People tell me I'm a good singer,' he told O'Leary. Pointing to Anne, he said: 'It's usually my mum.' Making a similar point to Harry's, O'Leary quipped: 'And they always say that!'

Harry agreed, and continued: 'Singing is what I want to do and if people who can make that happen for me don't think that I should be doing that then that's a major setback in my plans'. He admitted he was 'nervous' as well as 'excited'. As he departed to take to the stage, he was showered with kisses from his supporters. This was something he found 'a bit embarrassing,' he said. O'Leary remarked on the awkwardness of the moment, asking: 'Anyone else want to kiss him?' Lots of people soon would.

He turned away and walked onstage – his life was about to change for good. As he reached the centre of the stage, he said a cheeky hello to the judges. For Harry's audition they were Louis Walsh, Nicole Scherzinger and Simon Cowell; he also acknowledged the audience. He was asked by Cowell to say something about himself. 'Erm, I work in a bakery,' he said. 'I work there on Saturdays.' Not the most gripping of anecdotes but there was already something about Harry that made even patter like this charm people. Soon, there were squeals and screams of admiration in the audience.

On the stage, he sang 'Isn't She Lovely' by Stevie Wonder. At the end of the performance he was cheered loudly and he gave a sweet bow. Nicole Scherzinger was the first of the judges to speak. She told him: 'I'm really glad that we had the opportunity to hear you a cappella, 'cos we could really hear how great your voice is. For sixteen years old, you have a beautiful voice.' Louis Walsh was next: 'I agree with Nicole,' said the Irishman. 'However, I think you're so young. I don't think you have enough experience or confidence yet.' A cry of 'rubbish' came from someone, which the head judge duly picked up.

'Someone in the audience just said "rubbish" and I totally agree with them,' Simon Cowell said. 'Because the show is designed to find someone, whether you're fifteen, sixteen, seventeen – it doesn't matter. I think with a bit of vocal coaching you could actually be very good.'

With the general verdicts given, it was time for the judges to vote on whether he would proceed. This would be the moment of truth. Walsh, on the left of the panel, spoke first. 'Harry, for all the right reasons, I am going to say no.' There was shock, upset and not a little outrage among the audience in response. Cowell encouraged the audience to 'boo' as loud as they could. As they did so, Harry himself joined in with his own quick 'boo'. It was a moment of cheeky, playful defiance. A world away from the petulant responses of some who receive a negative on the show. It also showed a poise that not many X Factor hopefuls have. In fairness, he could afford to be laid-back about it because the other two judges had already given a strong indication they would put him through.

> There was shock, upset and not a little outrage among the audience in response. Cowell encouraged the audience to 'boo' as loud as they could. As they did so, Harry himself joined in with his own quick 'boo'.

And so it was: Walsh's 'no' vote was indeed quickly overruled by the fact that Cowell and Scherzinger both gave Harry a resounding 'yes'. The latter judge told him, 'I like you, Harry,' which cheered him no end. The moment he realized he had got through to boot camp was, he said, one of the best of his life to date. He was through – he returned to his family, friends and supporters backstage in triumph. They were bubbling over with excitement. Harry was so thrilled he began to be struck by a strange paranoia that somehow the decision would be changed. There was no chance of that happening, though it is slightly eerie that he almost forecast that judges can change their minds after giving a definitive verdict, as that would happen for him later in the series.

However, despite getting through, he had no idea what would happen next. The audition was broadcast some months after it was filmed. He had been forced to keep the details and his fate secret, so

He had been forced to keep the details and his fate secret, so he was excited when it was finally shown on ITV.

he was excited when it was finally shown on ITV. Text messages came flooding in from his friends to congratulate Harry. He got recognized by a stranger in a petrol station, which he found a very peculiar experience.

Another time a woman ran up to him in a park and asked for his autograph. When she handed Harry a pen, he asked whether she had a piece of paper. 'She just looked at me and got out her boobs,' he told *Fabulous* magazine. He'd soon get used to encounters like these. Nowadays, they are his everyday experience.

Meanwhile, four other young men who had also successfully auditioned on the show were making their own progress, which would intertwine their lives with Harry's, with all five of those lives ultimately changing. Over in Dublin, a young man called Niall Horan showed up to try his luck. He was living on pure adrenaline on the day, as the evening before his audition he had been so excited he could not get to sleep. He was staying the night with a cousin in Dublin but the more he tried to sleep the more he thought about the day ahead. He ended up in one of those cycles: the more he wanted to sleep the less able he was to do so. He knew it was important to get as much sleep as possible ahead of such an important, exciting and potentially draining day, but sleep just would not come. In the end he simply gave up trying to rest and got up to get ready. He chose to wear a checked shirt, blue jeans and trainers. He arrived at the Convention Centre Dublin, at Spencer Dock on the North Wall Quay, at the crack of dawn. He was so excited and nervous.

In his pre-audition interview he explained that he had sometimes been compared to Justin Bieber, adding that it was a comparison he enjoyed. Then, it was time to sing. As he walked onstage he greeted the crowd with a cheeky, 'All right, Dublin?' Then he told Walsh: 'I'm here today to be the best artist I can be in the world.'

He sang the Jason Mraz hit 'I'm Yours'. Cowell, who had heard so many people audition with this track over recent years, told Niall it was a lazy song to select and asked if he had a second song to perform instead. Niall said he did, and then sang it – 'So Sick' by Ne-Yo. There was some symbolism to this, as this was one of the songs that Justin Bieber sang at the Stratford Star talent contest that, ultimately, made him famous.

Katy Perry, who was a judge for the Irish leg of the auditions along with Cheryl Cole, told Niall: 'I think you're adorable! You've got charisma – I just think that maybe you should work on it. You're only sixteen: I started out when I was fifteen and I didn't make it until I was twenty-three.' A slightly mixed verdict, and one that made her final vote hard to predict. Cowell, too, was ambiguous. 'I think you're unprepared: I think you came with the wrong song, you're not as good as you thought you were, but I still like you,' he told Niall, who pulled a sweet expression in response to this.

Cheryl Cole said: 'Yeah, you're obviously adorable: you've got a lot of charm for a sixteen-year-old, but the song was too big for you, babe.' Everyone seemed to have a 'but' attached to any praise they gave Niall. The final judge to speak was Walsh. As a fellow Irishman and a man who specialized in managing boy bands, he would be, Niall hoped, more given to appreciate him. 'No, I think you've got something,' Walsh said. 'I think that people will absolutely like you because you're likeable.' Cowell immediately leaped on the comment, saying, with a sarcastic, withering tone: 'So, people will like him because he's likeable?'

When it came to voting time, it was hard to know what each judge would say. It was Cowell who spoke first. 'Well, I'm going to say yes,' he explained. Niall punched the air like a footballer, then kissed his hand and crossed himself. He was quickly deflated when Cole followed with a 'no'. Poor Niall looked absolutely gutted. Perry should have been next to speak but Walsh jumped the queue and told Niall: 'I'm going to say yes!' Contestants need a majority verdict from the panel, meaning that a yes from Perry was at this stage enough to send him through. 'So now,' explained a typically excitable Walsh, 'he needs three yeses!' Perry mimed a stabbing motion into her own neck, signifying how much pressure she now felt under. 'Of course you're in,' she said.

> Walsh said that he liked Zayn and Scherzinger said she felt he had something 'special'. Cowell was admiring, too, but added that he felt Zayn needed to become more ambitious.

For Zayn Malik, his *X Factor* 'journey' began with a long physical journey. To get from Bradford early enough to queue up for his audition he had to set off at 2 a.m. To prepare himself for such an early start, he had gone to bed at 4 p.m. the previous day. His uncle drove him down. Like Harry, Zayn auditioned in Manchester and sang a cappella, rather than to a backing track. He sung the Mario track, 'Let Me Love You'.

Walsh said that he liked Zayn and Scherzinger said she felt he had something 'special'. Cowell was admiring, too, but added that he felt Zayn needed to become more ambitious. Walsh and Scherzinger both said 'yes', and Zayn politely thanked them both. Cowell, too, put him through: 'Zayn, I'm going to say yes.'

Like Zayn, Louis Tomlinson left early for his audition. Or was it late? He left for Manchester around midnight. He and a friend slept in the car for a while when they arrived at the Manchester MEN Arena and began queuing properly around 4 a.m.

As he walked onto the stage he was suddenly a bit scared. As he wrote in the band's official book, his 'mouth went dry'. The first song he sang was the Scouting For Girls track 'Elvis Ain't Dead'. This song is typical of the bouncy indie-pop of the band. Before Louis could really get into his stride with the song he was stopped by Cowell, who felt that it would be better if Louis tried another track. For his second track Louis had selected and rehearsed a far tamer song – 'Hey There Delilah' by the Plain White T's.

When it came time for the verdicts, Louis' namesake Walsh told him: 'Louis – I'm saying yes.' Scherzinger echoed this, exclaiming: 'I'm saying yes.' Could Louis complete the set with a positive from Cowell? He could. 'You've got three yeses,' said the head judge.

> To add to the overall performance, he clicked the beat of the song with his fingers and even winked cheekily at Cole.

For Liam Payne, 2010 was to be his second experience auditioning for the show. In 2008, he turned up to audition. 'I'm here to win,' he told the judges, throwing down the gauntlet from the off. 'A lot of people have told me I'm a good singer and that I've got the X Factor – but I don't really know what the X Factor is and I believe you guys do.' It was a measured and shrewd opening line. Cowell in particular admires those whose ambitions are high, but equally dislikes any sense of delusion or desperation. Liam had pitched himself well. He sang the song 'Fly Me To The Moon' and did so well. To add to the overall performance, he clicked the beat of the song with his fingers and even winked cheekily at Cole. She appreciated the moment and

It was Cowell who spoke first. He said he saw 'potential' in Liam but simultaneously felt he lacked 'a bit of grit, a bit of emotion'.

beamed back in approval. In years to come this brief exchange would take on a whole new meaning.

When it was time for the judges' verdicts, it was Cowell's opinion that Liam was most interested in. He was more than a bit in awe of the head judge and was dying to receive his widely coveted nod of approval. Liam knew that Cowell, who can be quite cutting at times, did not offer anyone praise lightly. It was Cowell who spoke first. He said he saw 'potential' in Liam but simultaneously felt he lacked 'a bit of grit, a bit of emotion'. Cole said she liked Liam and, in contrast to Cowell, was impressed by the 'charisma' he showed. Walsh, too, was charmed. 'I think he could do really well,' said the Irishman.

Cowell then spoke again. He told Liam he was 'a young guy, good-looking – people will like you', but added that there was 'twenty per cent missing for me at the moment'. However, Liam argued back and stood his ground and got put through.

At boot camp, he got more experience of performing and also of the plot twists that have become such a part of the show. When Liam stood alongside his fellow contestants, he listened intently to Cowell's words. 'Whatever happens, you can leave with your heads held high,' the head judge told them, but added: 'It's bad news.' Even as they left the stage, Liam momentarily turned back to the judges. Perhaps he was hoping for a last-moment twist. Backstage, he was distraught. He said he thought he had done enough to progress, and said: 'I feel like something's been taken away from me.' The judges were then shown changing their minds about Liam. 'I'm telling you, I think this kid's got a shot,' said Cowell.

A producer was sent to grab Liam and tell him the judges wanted him to return to the stage. Naturally, he looked shocked.

He had watched the show in past series and knew that there were always a few 'twists' to ramp up the drama. While he hoped he was returning to the stage to be told he was back in the competition, he knew he could not afford to count on anything. 'I'm just confused,' he said. Cowell broke the silence when Liam appeared on the stage, looking a little sheepish. 'I don't often do this, but it was such a close call,' Cowell began. Liam then interrupted to make a final plea for himself: 'I want to take it all the way, Simon.'

Naturally, he looked shocked. He had watched the show in past series and knew that there were always a few 'twists' to ramp up the drama.

'I know you do,' Cowell replied, 'and the other thing I want to say to you is: "We've changed our minds."' At the judges' houses in Barbados, he sang the Take That ballad 'A Million Love Songs' and 'Hero' by Enrique Iglesias. He was dressed all in white and looked very much the part of an angelic pop star. After he finished Sinitta, who was Simon's guest judge, seemed smitten. 'Love him,' she said. 'He has such a cute face — nice little voice as well.' But when it came to the verdicts, Cowell told Liam: 'You look almost like the perfect pop star. I've made a decision — it's bad news.' Again, Liam tried to argue his case. This time, though, there would be no redemption — he was out.

But when he returned two years later, it was a very different story. It was Cowell who Liam first addressed on taking the stage. 'How you doing, Simon, you all right?' he asked casually. 'Haven't seen you in a long time!' He then confirmed it had been two years since he last auditioned, at which point he 'made it through to Simon's house in Barbados'. He was coming across as very relaxed and confident. He sang 'Cry Me a River' by Michael Bublé as the track rang out behind him.

At verdict time, each of the three judges' 'yes' vote thrilled him. None more so, of course, than Cowell's final verdict. 'Based on talent – absolutely incredible,' he told Liam. 'One massive, fat, almighty yes.' No wonder Liam sank almost all the way to the floor with joy. It was an emotional moment: one could almost see the disappointment of his 2008 rejection lift from his young shoulders. The other four boys had all got through and they were all about to become a huge part of Harry's life. But first, they all had to endure the rigours of the boot-camp phase.

At boot camp, things were rough before they were smooth. 'I met them as solo artists to begin with,' Cowell later told *Rolling Stone* magazine. 'Each of them individually had very good auditions.' Mentioning Harry and Liam, he added: 'We had high hopes for two or three of them in particular, and then it all kind of fell apart at one of the latter stages.'

The boot-camp phase was held at Wembley Arena over five days in July 2010. A total of 211 acts had made it through the auditions phase to this stage. From the first day of boot camp, on 22 July, it was clear that proceedings would be just as brutal as in past series of *The X Factor*. Each of the four categories – Boys, Girls, Over-25s and Groups – were given a different song to prepare. Harry and the others in the boys' category were given Michael Jackson's 'Man in the Mirror'.

'We had high hopes for two or three of them in particular, and then it all kind of fell apart at one of the latter stages.'

Harry was shocked when the judges gathered all the contestants, and Cowell told them what was at stake on day one of boot camp. 'By the end of the day, half of you are going home,' Cowell told them. Harry gulped. 'Today, you're going to be put in your categories and you're going to sing one song. There are literally no second chances today.' Luckily for Harry, his version of 'Man in the Mirror' was good enough to see him through.

His ambition was truly fired up. The more hurdles he successfully negotiated, the greater and more intense his determination became. He told the cameras: 'As you go through boot camp you kind of realize how big the prize is, so being here the last few days has made me realize how much I wanna stay – I really don't want to go home now.'

On the third day of boot camp the contestants were handed a list of forty songs from which to choose one to sing. Harry chose 'Stop Crying Your Heart Out' by Oasis. As he and the rest of the boys took to the stage to discover who had made it through to judges' houses, he could hardly have been more nervous. Name after name was announced as going through but somehow Harry's was never announced. Then it got down to just two names left. Harry wished one of them would be him but the final two names called out were those of Matt Cardle and Tom Richards. 'That's it, guys – I'm really sorry,' said Cowell.

When a camera approached him backstage for his reaction, Harry said he was 'really gutted' and he looked it. However, Cowell was having second thoughts. 'I had a bad feeling that maybe we shouldn't have lost them and maybe there was something else we should do with them,' he explained later. 'And this is when the idea came about that we should see if they could work as a group.' Whether the decision was made on the spur of that moment or whether it had been more premeditated, it was now time to act on it.

The boys were called back to the stage along with a group of girls who went on to form the group Belle Amie. As Cowell looked at Harry and the other four boys, he had no doubt. 'The minute they stood there for the first time together – it was a weird feeling,' he told *Rolling Stone* later. 'They just looked like a group at that point.' Cowell told them, 'We've decided to put you both through to the judges' houses.' Harry sank to his knees in victory and disbelief. 'Guys, guys, girls, girls – this is a lifeline: you've got to work ten, twelve, fourteen hours a day, every single day, and take this opportunity,' he told them. 'You've got a real shot here, guys.' Backstage, Harry spoke for all five when he told O'Leary: 'I went from the worst feeling in my life to the best.'

For judges' houses, Harry and the band would fly to Marbella in Spain to perform in front of Cowell. For the successful acts in this stage of the process the prize is huge: a place in the live shows. The band sang 'Torn' by Natalie Imbruglia. Liam led the vocals during the first verse, Harry took the bridge and then all five sang during the chorus. As they swung their hips during the final chorus, the band suddenly looked surprisingly convincing as a unit, considering the tender age of both the band and its individuals. At the end of the song Cowell gave nothing away to the band, merely saying: 'See you later.' But inside he was already convinced. *Rolling Stone* asked Simon when he realized they would be successful, and Cowell confirmed that it was almost instant. 'When they came to my house in Spain and performed, after about a millionth of a second,' he said. 'I tried to keep a straight face for a bit of drama for the show.'

He kept that drama going when it came time to tell the band the news. 'My head is saying it's a risk and my heart is saying that you deserve a shot,' he told them, making sure he inserted plenty of dramatic pauses to up the tension. 'And that's why it's been difficult, so I've made a decision. Guys, I've gone with my heart – you're through!' The roar that came from the boys as they celebrated said it all. They then ran to celebrate with Cowell – Harry the first to arrive in the arms of their mentor. 'I am so impressed with all of you, I mean that,' Cowell told them. It was time for the live shows.

* * *

Harry said that moving into the *X Factor* house was 'cool'. The band had a 'tiny' room but Harry said he didn't mind, even when it

> In years gone by, Cowell had tended to give his boy bands predictable ballads, complete with the hackneyed key change. But the more imaginative song choice had been a risk worth taking.

got 'grotty'. Behind the scenes, Harry was regularly stripping off. He has said that he finds getting naked 'liberating'. It had been since he was at school, when he would often moon people. He would walk round the X Factor house either totally naked, or clad in just a gold snake-print thong, which he wore for a laugh. Plenty of One Direction's fans would have been very happy to see Harry on those occasions.

Ahead of their first live show performance Harry was so nervous he threw up. As the band appeared and sang the song, he showed his nerves with an intense, almost aggressive stage presence. As he thumped his shoulder to the beat his facial expression tried, unsuccessfully, to conceal his nerves. The band sang 'Viva La Vida' by Coldplay, not a song many would have predicted they would have sung. In years gone by, Cowell had tended to give his boy bands predictable ballads, complete with the hackneyed key change. But the more imaginative song choice had been a risk worth taking.

As the crowd applauded, Cowell beamed with avuncular pride. Louis Walsh told them: 'Wow guys, when I heard you were going to do Coldplay I thought it was a big, big risk! I love what you did with the song – you totally made it your own. Boys, I think potentially you could be the next big boy band, but you have a lot of work to do.' He added, with a sting: 'But Simon Cowell, I'm not sure about the styling! Did you have a stylist?' Dannii Minogue said: 'That song was fantastic and you did make it your own.' Cole said: 'I reckon the girls will be going crazy for you, but you need a little bit more time to develop as a group, that's all. Just a little bit more time.' Cowell said: 'It was brilliant, guys.' Harry said: 'It was the best experience of all of our lives.' He and his bandmates celebrated with aplomb when they got through – it had been a great week.

The week leading up to their performance in the second round was tough for the band because Harry had another attack of nerves during the soundcheck. He could not breathe properly and felt like he was going to be sick again. When it came to the performance of 'My Life Would Suck Without You' by Kelly Clarkson, all was well. Afterwards, Minogue said: 'I have to say that you're five heart–throbs. You look great together and Harry, whatever nerves you have, I'm sure your friends and you will stick together.'

There were smiles all round when Cole said: 'I can't even cope with how cute you are. Seriously, I can't!' Harry put his hands together in a praying motion – as if his prayers had just been answered. Cowell said: 'Let me tell you, you are the most exciting pop band in the country today. I'm being serious – there is something absolutely right.' As the audience cheered Cowell's words,

> There were smiles all round when Cole said: 'I can't even cope with how cute you are. Seriously, I can't!'

Harry theatrically urged them to cheer louder. There was even louder cheering and celebrations galore when One Direction were again sent through by the public vote.

In week three they sang 'Nobody Knows' by Pink. The most interesting part of the performance was the way the power was shifting. Previously, Liam had been the undoubted frontman in the band's performances, but this time Harry sang alone in parts. While Liam was still very much the lead member, Harry's confidence was rising and, with it, so too was his place in the One Direction pecking order. Afterwards, Cole said: 'You know what, guys, let me just put this out there: you are my guilty pleasure! I've got to tell you, apart from it being a great performance, I thought vocally, you've really, really made some really huge improvements.' Backstage after they had performed, Harry spoke with excitement about another week of praise from the judges. 'The comments were absolutely brilliant,' he beamed. 'For us to keep proceeding in the competition, we have to get better every week.'

The following week, there was another crucial moment in the power evolution between Harry and Liam. Harry stood in the centre of the line-up but it was Liam who again led the vocals. Cowell told them: 'What I really admire about you guys is I know people are under pressure when you go into a competition like this. You've got to remember you're sixteen, seventeen years old. The way you've conducted yourselves: don't believe the hype – work hard, rehearse. Honestly, it's a total pleasure working with you lot.' On the following night's show, Harry said: 'Last night felt brilliant. We got a real chance to show off our vocals and hopefully the fans at home will vote and keep us in because we really don't want to go home now.'

The next week – after a pre-show VT that included some gratuitous scenes of Harry in just his underwear – they appeared on the stage to sing the Kim Wilde hit, 'Kids in America'. Harry was again centre stage. The way he leaped up at the end of the song, landing with a defiant thump on the final note, summed up their confidence. Simon justified that confidence when he told Harry and the band: 'That was without question your best performance by a mile.'

The following week was Elton John week. One Direction sang 'Something About the Way You Look Tonight'. Harry, standing in the centre of the line-up, contributed his most significant solo of the series to date. The show's producers had noted the growing frenzy around him and, with his poise growing week on week, were moving him to a more leading role in the band. As he began his first line, the screams and howls of the audience showed this was a popular move.

Again, the judges were full of praise. Cowell said: 'Guys, I want to say something, okay? This is the first time in all the years of *X Factor* where I genuinely believe a group are going to win this competition. Guys, congratulations.'

For the Beatles week, they sang an uptempo version of 'All You Need is Love'. Harry again took plenty of the vocals, including an excited ad lib of 'Come on!' What had started as a quiet performance ended in rapture, with dancers behind the band bouncing up and down.

However, it was in the following week – the rock week – that things started to really change for Harry. This was the week that his ascendancy within the band's pecking order really began to become noticeable. Although Liam still took plenty of the vocals for their opening track of the two-song night, the very choice of song was Harry's. They sang 'Summer of '69', a song Harry had sung as a boy. With the song choice presented on air as entirely Harry's doing, he was getting plenty of attention. Already, it had been reported that Harry had come up with the name of the band, after commenting that they were all 'headed in one direction'. He also led the band on their mid-

> It had been reported that Harry had come up with the name of the band, after commenting that they were all 'headed in one direction'.

song walkabout and as they returned to the stage it was he who was positioned in the middle for the song's conclusion. It was as if a changing of the musical guard was happening. Afterwards, Cowell contributed to the sense of elevation around Harry. 'I had nothing to do with this song choice – Harry chose the song, great choice of song,' he said. As Harry beamed his winning smile, he was congratulated by his bandmates, with Niall even toying with Harry's famous curly locks.

However, Liam did not seem overjoyed about all this. Perhaps feeling relegated by the attention and increasing prominence of Harry, he was notably long-faced and seemed downcast as O'Leary continued the Harry lovefest. 'Trust me, the last thing we should be doing is bigging Harry up any more than we already big him up,' quipped the host.

For the second song, they performed 'You Are So Beautiful'. As Harry, centre stage, tenderly sang his lines, the camera zooming close on his boyish face, his eyes the definition of boy-band dolefulness, it was difficult to argue with the producers' decision to increasingly focus on him. All in all the band had done more than enough to get through to the semi-finals, where they sang Rihanna's 'Only Girl (in the World)'. Cowell was very effusive in his praise. 'I've got to tell you guys, I know this is going to sound a bit biased but I thought

> 'I thought this song was absolutely perfect for you because it is exactly what I liked about them – they didn't take the safe option.'

this song was absolutely perfect for you because it is exactly what I liked about them – they didn't take the safe option,' he said. 'They chose something completely different: they had the guts to do it ... Can I just say, you hear all the applause and people at home might think you're safe but nobody is safe in this competition and I would urge anyone, please, if they want to see these boys in the final, please pick up the phone and vote for them because they deserve it.'

Enough people did indeed pick up the phone and vote for them and they were through to the final. Along with Matt Cardle, Cher Lloyd and Rebecca Ferguson, they would battle it out to be crowned X Factor champion. Was a band about to win the show for the first time?

At the final, many assumed that One Direction would romp home and become the first band to win the contest. The feeling was that they were the standout act of the competition. Some even suggested that the show might be somehow 'fixed' in their favour. However, a glimpse of what was to come was hinted at in a poll published in the *Sun* newspaper on the morning of the final. The survey put Harry and the boys in a distant third behind Ferguson and the poll's predicted winner, Cardle. During the week, in the build-up to the final, the band had played a short live concert in Liam's hometown, Wolverhampton. Harry added that it was 'really exciting for us to think we're going to be doing loads of little gigs like that and some to bigger crowds than that'.

> It was 'really exciting for us to think we're going to be doing loads of little gigs like that and some to bigger crowds than that.'

On the night, the nerves kicked in but Harry and the guys still put in a strong performance. After they sang 'Your Song' by Elton John, Louis Walsh was as impressed as ever: 'Hey One Direction, you're in the final – I hope you're here tomorrow night,' he said. 'It's amazing how five guys have gelled so well. I know you're all best friends. I've never seen a band cause so much hysteria so early in their career. I definitely think that you've got an amazing future. Niall, everybody in Ireland must vote for Niall, yes!'

Minogue echoed Walsh. 'Guys, you have worked so hard in this competition – you were thrown together, you deserve to be here and I'd love to see you in the final tomorrow,' she said. Cowell said that the first two performances by One Direction's rivals Cardle and Ferguson were 'so good' that his 'heart was sinking' over his band's potential. However, he said, the band 'gave it one thousand per cent' and added 'it's been an absolute pleasure working with you'. Lest his contribution sound like an obituary for the band's *X Factor* experience, he added: 'I really hope people bother to pick up the phone, put you through to tomorrow because you deserve to be there.'

Next up, it was time for the band to sing their duets with established pop icons. Cardle sang with Rihanna, Lloyd with will.i.am of the Black Eyed Peas and Ferguson with Christina Aguilera. These were prestigious artists, particularly Cardle's partner. However, One Direction felt that they had the pick of the lot – Robbie Williams. The man who had influenced them so much was about to join them to sing on prime-time television.

Together, they sang Robbie's classic hit, 'She's the One'. Each of the boys looked so happy it was impossible for viewers' hearts not to melt. As his successful duet with One Direction came to an end, he shouted, 'The lads – One Direction! Phone in!' and then all six disappeared briefly into a group hug. Robbie even lifted Niall into the air. Louis said he was 'an absolutely massive Robbie fan – thank you so much for doing this with us'. Robbie casually replied, 'Oh it's a pleasure – you guys rock!' Harry, looking more serious than ever, spoke of the 'pleasure it had been to sing with Robbie'. Cowell described Robbie as 'a great friend to the show – very, very generous with his time and he's made these boys' night of their lives'.

* * *

The following night, Harry and the band put in what would be their final performance of the series: One Direction sang 'Torn'. As the song they had sung at judges' houses, this was an emotional choice. It reminded the lads themselves, as well as – crucially – the audience, how far they had come. Their opponents, Cardle and Ferguson, sang Katy Perry's 'Firework' and the Eurythmics' 'Sweet Dreams' respectively. The next count of the votes would eliminate one of the three, before the final two would go through to sing what would be their putative winners' single. Following further voting, the winner would then be crowned.

As the judges gave their verdicts, Harry might have noticed that some of what they said sounded like they believed that the band was about to be voted out. The final judges' verdicts for the band were all upbeat, but were – for the most part – phrased in expectation that this was the end of the road in the competition. Walsh told them: 'You've got brilliant chemistry, I love the harmonies. I love the song choice and we've got five new pop stars!' Minogue added: 'Guys, you've done all the right things to make your place here in the final. That was a fantastic performance. Whatever happens tonight, I'm sure you guys are going to go on and release records and be the next big band.' Cole in particular sounded a conclusive note, saying: 'It's been so lovely to watch you guys from your first audition. To think that was only a few months ago! I really believe that you've got a massive future ahead of you and I wanna say "thank you" for being such lovely guys to be around.' Only Cowell, perhaps predictably, spoke of the band surviving the next cull and winning the show. 'Let's be clear: anyone who comes into this final has got a great chance of bettering their future,' he said. 'But this is a competition and in terms of the competition, in terms of who's worked the hardest, who I think deserves to win based on the future of something we haven't seen before. I would love to hear your names read out at the end of the competition – because I think you deserve it.' But it was not to be. With Cardle and Minogue on the left of the stage and Ferguson and Cheryl on the right, One Direction were in the middle, flanked by Cowell. Complete with the customary,

> 'You've got brilliant chemistry, I love the harmonies. I love the song choice and we've got five new pop stars!'

agonizing dramatic pauses, O'Leary announced that first Cardle and then Ferguson were through, which knocked One Direction out of the remainder of the contest. Cowell was the first to react to the disappointing news. He looked distraught, almost angry, as he turned his back on proceedings. It was the body language of disgust. The boys looked absolutely devastated and, unlike at boot camp, there was not to be a sudden change of mind.

Later, it would be revealed that Harry and the boys had in fact come either third or fourth in the voting most weeks during the live shows. Therefore, their third-place finish was about right; but on the night it seemed a huge shock.

After Cardle was named the winner, the frenzied celebrations led to a few moments of comedy and, for Harry, a truly iconic moment. Amid the chaos, Cardle managed to accidentally knock his mentor Dannii Minogue in the face. Then, as O'Leary wrapped up the evening

The camera caught Harry whispering something to the triumphant Cardle. Not everybody noticed what Harry had said but some eagle-eyed viewers thought that they did.

and the series itself, the camera caught Harry whispering something to the triumphant Cardle. Not everybody noticed what Harry had said but some eagle-eyed viewers thought that they did.

Within moments, Twitter was awash with messages speculating that what Harry had said was: 'Just think how much pussy you're going to get.' This theory was picked up by the mainstream media and provoked a combination of outrage, amusement and approval from differing sectors of the British public. Though Harry initially declined to comment publicly over what he had said, he would in time confirm that he had indeed made the bawdy remark, but not before the subject had been dubbed 'pussygate'. In the meantime, his mother was so angry that she would ground him when he got home.

Later in the evening of the final, and looking back over the series, Harry struck a more wholesome tone. 'When we walked in and saw the studio for the first time, then when us five stood behind the doors for the first time on the live show, for that first song – for me that was the best moment. That was where we were actually doing it, the real thing, for the first time. That was a big moment.'

But that 'pussy' comment was also a big moment, whether Harry wanted it to be or not. In branding terms, it served him well. It gave his image a cheeky, Lothario flavour that many members of boy bands would kill for. Whether he intended for lip-readers to notice his comment, or whether it was just a spontaneous comment he never meant anyone to notice, there was a genius to it. Cardle may have won the series but One Direction were clearly the true victors. And of those true victors, Harry was the champion.

CHAPTER THREE

THE RISE AND RISE OF ONE DIRECTION

After the pain of elimination came the joy of Harry's new chapter. He and the band were called to a private meeting with Simon Cowell. 'I've made a decision,' he told them, then cheekily embarked on a trademark dramatic pause. Having upped the ante with his pause, he told them what that decision was: he was going to sign them up to his division of Sony. The man Harry called 'Uncle Simon' had shown that, even when the cameras are not trained on him, he cannot resist leaving people hanging on his decisions. When his decisions are frequently of such a monumental nature, it must be hard to resist hamming it up a bit, even if that leaves hopefuls almost breathless with anticipation.

With a broad smile that revealed his shimmering Hollywood fangs, Cowell told the band: 'You have to enjoy yourselves. You're going to make a lot of money, but you have to enjoy every single minute of it.' Harry absolutely drank up these words.

Though the received wisdom had been that Cowell would of course sign the band whether they won *The X Factor* or not, Harry and his bandmates had never taken that for granted. They knew that the entertainment industry is a ruthless one in which tough decisions are made regardless of the feelings of the human beings concerned.

As they got the news they had longed to hear, the emotions got so strong that Harry burst into tears, his composed persona utterly abandoned in the excitement of the moment. Then he and the others rushed to phone their parents to tell them the news.

> Emotions got so strong that Harry burst into tears, his composed persona utterly abandoned in the excitement of the moment.

Like many performers, the boys were keen to make their parents proud. It felt amazing to tell them what had happened.

Though Harry did not realize this straight away, Cowell had almost made a noteworthy sacrifice. He felt that he had such a promising prospect on his hands that he invited other divisions of Sony to make their own presentations to him before he decided where to send the boys. Rather than automatically signing them to his division, he was willing to consider handing them elsewhere. He explained why to *Rolling Stone*: 'This was such an important signing, we let three or four of the Sony labels make a presentation,' he said. 'I didn't automatically give it to my own label. I thought, "This is so important, if somebody can come up with a better idea ..." I was actually willing to pass them along to another division of Sony because I thought the group were that important.'

Pumped full of excitement, the band then went their separate ways for Christmas. There would be a short break with their families before the serious work began. But even during this break, which was designed to be the quiet before the storm, Harry got a small glimpse of how his life was about to change. He noted an almost perpetual gathering of fans near his family home. This was his first encounter with such intrusive fandom: he found himself worrying about them out there in the winter air. He thought they might end up catching a cold and he didn't want them to get ill waiting for him. Zayn had his own experience during this time when he brought a shopping centre to a virtual standstill within a minute or two of him first being recognized. The bandmates all swapped notes via text message.

Harry was relieved to be able to spend time with his friends over Christmas because he had been gripped by a fear that they might think he had changed, or got above his station, with his new-found fame. He tried to make as much time for them as possible. During the live show period of *The X Factor*, his friends would often text Harry and sometimes he would be so busy and distracted that he would forget to reply. He would be reading a text and then he'd suddenly be rushed off to the next part of the process, so he'd forget to text back. So he was relieved when he met up with friends over the Christmas break and they'd tell him that he hadn't changed at all. This was music to Harry's ears.

At times he has, he says, encountered 'jealousy' from some people in his life, and some people have made unpleasant remarks and distanced themselves from him. Some of these people were cold to Harry when he tried to speak to them about the problem. In the end, he concluded, it was not he who had changed but their attitude towards him.

As his fame and fortune developed, Harry had dilemmas when

dealing with people. A naturally generous character, he liked the idea of treating his friends to something nice when they met up. At the same time, though, he was mindful that this could appear flash.

Similarly, as the band became surrounded by a team of assistants, he would find that basic things would be done for him. However, as far as Harry was concerned, he was capable of fetching his own bottle of water or snack. He didn't want to become that diva who demands that their assistants peel their every grape for them. As he says, Anne would never have let him become such a character, anyway. Were he to ask her to fetch him a glass of water, he said, she would have replied: 'You know where the glasses are.' For Harry, trying to keep his feet on the ground as his fame soared higher has been a major preoccupation and continues to be to this day.

With Christmas and New Year over, it was time for the work to begin. But for Harry, it didn't really feel like work. At sixteen, he might have been returning to school or continuing college, heading out in the dark, cold mornings to another day in the classroom. If he had not succeeded at his opening *X Factor* audition, this would almost certainly have been his fate. Instead, he was off to California.

In January 2011, he and the band began recording their debut album. They flew to LA, where they began work with Moroccan-Swedish producer RedOne. In total, they spent five days in Los Angeles – the capital of the entertainment industry. The sun was shining and Harry couldn't stop smiling. He had been unable to believe that he was going there. He remembered that when he was told that was their next destination, his mouth fell open. The time was spent in a combination of work – including a recording session in a studio and a meeting with leading producer Max Martin – sightseeing and shopping.

Already unconsciously adopting California-speak, Harry reported back that he found Los Angeles 'something else'. Everyone he saw seemed to either be, or look like, a celebrity. He loved how polite service staff were out there and said he would almost feel like inviting them to sit down and join him for the meal. In downtime, he went and bought a tonne of T-shirts from Abercrombie and Fitch and also relaxed by the pool at their hotel, the luxury W Hotel. The whole experience had been as glamorous and sunny as he had hoped.

* * *

When they returned to the UK, the band were given another class in their crash course in fame – when they arrived at Heathrow Airport, Harry and the boys were confronted with hundreds of screaming fans. Security staff had to grab the boys and whizz them to a police van, just to avoid them being mobbed by the fans. It was a crazy experience.

Amusingly, Ronan Keating, the former Boyzone lead singer, a heart-throb back in the 1990s, was also arriving around the same time. Once upon a time he had faced scenes such as this. He wrote on Twitter: 'Just landed at heathrow and when I walked out there were hundreds of screaming fans sadly not for me HaHa. One direction were on flight. X' [sic]. Still, the experience will have brought back fond memories for Keating and, more pertinently, showed Harry what was in store for him.

First on the agenda when the band returned was the X Factor tour. Preparations began with the band moving into a hotel together, another move to build the band vibe. Rarely does a band have such huge popularity after such a brief time together, so it was important from the management's point of view that the dynamic between Harry and the rest of the group was strong.

The boys were truly put through their paces in the days before the tour – they had to learn new dance moves and also rehearse some onstage banter for between the songs. The rehearsals and the drilling were serious and testing: they went over some parts of their slot more than twenty times. These were tough days at the Light Structures venue in Wakefield. Harry was discovering how much hard work was involved with being in a band. The tour was also a chance for the band to reunite and bond with the other finalists from *The X Factor*. On the tour they shared a dressing room with the other male acts. This meant that they were reunited with Cardle and the other contestants from the show, including Wagner. It made for a crowded and energy-filled room as they laughed, remembering the funny times during the series and also discussing what was on the horizon in their respective futures. Clearly, Harry's was already looking rather different to, say, Wagner's. However, Harry was happy to play a prank on Wagner. He told *3AM* that one night after the Brazilian had fallen asleep, he arranged teddy bears all round him and snapped a photo. 'Picking the best pranks is the hardest bit,' he added.

After each show they would head to that city's hotel, often pouring themselves into the bar to party the rest of the night away. On two separate occasions they ended up having huge 'fruit fights'. The first, in Sheffield, lasted for five minutes. It kicked off when Louis casually tried to launch an apple core into the bin. Before they knew it, fruit was flying through the air. There was a 'second leg' fruit fight in Liverpool. They were having such a laugh, no wonder Harry said that he never wanted the tour to end.

As for the shows themselves, they were a true buzz for Harry. Onstage, he simply loved every moment. From the opening night in Birmingham, when the deafening noise from the 12,000-strong crowd that greeted the band blew the boys away, through the other cities, including in Ireland, it was an experience he would never forget. Naturally, it also served as a useful apprenticeship for the touring experience. In the future, they would fill venues just as large as, and even larger than, those on the X Factor tour. Generally, successful bands slowly build their live career from small venues to medium-sized and then the biggies, rather than selling out massive arenas on their first tour. So it was of enormous help that they had already had these tasters of being onstage in front of such enormous and noisy fans.

The deafening noise from the 12,000-strong crowd that greeted the band blew the boys away.

Manchester was a particular highlight for him. With his friends and family in the audience, it felt like a special night. He says the show in Dublin was 'crazy' and he also remembers the Newcastle gig, because his mum had travelled to that one, too. The band were singing five tracks at the shows – the only act other than the winner, Cardle, to have so many songs. They would perform 'Kids in America', 'Only Girl (in the World)', 'Forever Young', 'Chasing Cars' and 'My Life Would Suck Without You'. Every show felt 'incredible' to Harry, he said.

There was so much fun to be had. Harry made sure to tease Liam when his trousers ripped onstage. It was always during their rendition of 'Forever Young' that his 'wardrobe malfunction' occurred. None of the screaming girls in the crowd were particularly upset to see more than expected of Liam's lower regions. At the wrap party, which was held after the final performance in a hotel nightclub, the crew, management and artists fondly bid farewell to the tour and each other. The tour had established that the biggest party animals of the band were Harry and Louis, although most observers agreed that Louis probably pipped Harry for the championship.

Meanwhile, the commercial potential of the band was being made clear to Harry. An early deal was for them to film a television advertisement for the Nintendo DS Pokémon product. The advertisement was hardly strenuous work for the band. It was shot in a hotel room and essentially just featured them playing around. Although it was easy work for nice money, these sorts of projects began to bring home to Harry that part of being a pop star of such stature meant you were something of a 'cash cow' for big companies. For a lad who had worked in a bakery for a few quid, this was quite a change.

Another promotional project they were involved with at this time was the release of their first official book, *Forever Young*. Frenzied signing appearances helped push sales of the title ever higher – it ended up quite a hit in the bestseller charts. Unofficial books were also published in the months after the series, so Harry and the guys found themselves in a curious position: they were a pop band with more books than records to their names.

They went on a signing tour for the book, during which Harry wore some eye-catching T-shirts. One read 'Harry hearts Louis' – a slogan that would start the ball rolling on rumours that the two band members were an item. As we will see, this rumour would go on to become something of a pain to both of them – particularly Tomlinson. Another T-shirt he wore said: 'Tofu Guys Don't Eat Meat'. There could be little arguing with that.

Soon, it would be time to begin redressing that books/records ratio by recording their first album. First, though, it was time for another break. Harry and Louis went skiing in Courchevel in the French Alps. They each took a friend. Because Harry was new to skiing he needed some help and he got it from Louis.

Louis' late mother, Johanna, was pleased to see the blossoming friendship between Harry and her son. 'I really like Harry,' she said. 'I liked him from the first day I met him. They definitely do have a really strong bond. It's not a fabricated thing; it's not contrived. It's not something they thought they'd do to see if they could get any mileage out of it. They're like brothers. They genuinely respect and love each other.'

During the skiing trip there was an embarrassing moment when some fellow tourists asked for a photograph. Louis takes up the story. 'One time Harry and I were skiing together when a girl and a guy came up to us with a camera,' he told Seventeen. 'We assumed they were going to ask us for a photo so we stood there with our arms around each other, posing. They said: "No, we want you to take a photo of us!" It was embarrassing.'

Then it was time for the band to record their debut single. Harry's ambitions for their first release were high. Having watched in wonder as the Black Eyed Peas' single 'I Gotta Feeling' became the single of the summer of 2009, Harry wanted nothing less for the One Direction opener – a song 'everyone would remember'. It speaks volumes for Harry, who had a matter of months earlier been an unknown kid working in a bakery, that he thought in such ambitious and iconic terms. While his bandmates continued to emit an attitude of overexcited kids, willing to go along with whatever came the band's way, Harry was thinking strategically and big. He was, in other words, thinking like a star.

The song that had been carefully chosen for them was 'What Makes You Beautiful'. It begins with a brief, staccato guitar riff. The riff is uptempo, with an almost cheeky feel to it, reminiscent of the early material of McFly. Then the sound of a drumstick on a cymbal ushers in the first verse and Liam's voice comes in: it's deep and semi-raunchy in tone, with a hint of an American accent – perhaps a hangover from the time spent in LA after The X Factor.

The backing track becomes richer for the bridge, which is sung by Harry. His soulful, dreamy voice is at its best as he leads the track to its explosive chorus. He truly shows his effortless star quality here. The impish, noisy chorus is domineering to the imagination of the listener. Even before the almost addictively catchy 'you don't know-oh-oh' comes about, one is hooked. The idea of the boys being 'overwhelmed' by the girl flicking her hair prompts the listener to conjure an arresting image.

That classic pop trick of a 'na na na na' chant is included in the song before the a cappella middle eight, which Harry sings. It is an unexpected moment of quiet and calm – all the better to precede the final chorus, which crashes in supremely. A song this fun and wild should not end quietly – and it does not. Instead, a final 'That's what makes you beautiful' from Harry closes the three minutes and eighteen seconds of pop perfection.

'What Makes You Beautiful' has a pop chart full of identifiable influences. As well as the aforementioned tinge of McFly, there are also hints of American pop giants NSYNC, 1970s prog-rock Pink Floyd and the Mexican pop-folk classic 'La Bamba'. The styles of Example and Calvin Harris have also been cited by some critics. Many

> A song this fun and wild should not end quietly – and it does not.

pundits also noted a connection between the opening riff and that of the Grease track, 'Summer Lovin''. It was proving to be quite the case of spot the influence.

But what a track it is. Written by Rami Yacoub, Carl Falk and Savan Kotecha – who between them have composed for Westlife, Britney Spears, Nicki Minaj, Usher and Celine Dion – it was, in truth, pretty much teen pop gold. Musically, its chord progression is bright and its production – masterminded by Yacoub and Falk – is simple. Praise must go to those behind the track as well as those who selected it for One Direction: songs such as this, which so perfectly capture and define the spirit of teenage pop, might sound easy to produce but they are not. Never had a generation of girls been more inclined to flip their hair.

Showing again his precocious industry sass, Harry said: 'When we were recording in the studio we knew instantly that we wanted this track to be our first single.' He added, 'I think for us we wanted to release something that wasn't cheesy but it was fun. It kind of represented us, I think it took us a while to find it but I think we found the right song.'

It was released on 11 September 2011 and the critics were impressed. Summing up the theme of the song as one that showed that the band's 'favourite sort' of lady is 'That endangered breed who are visually stunning but aren't aware of it', *Digital Spy*'s Robert Copsey heaped praise on the track. Giving it four out of five stars, he declared it a cross between Pink and McFly, concluding: 'Like a Forever Friends bear from your high school crush, it's adorable, completely innocent and bound to cause a stir among your mates.'

A less expected champion of it was the *NME* magazine, which generally prefers its music less pop and more indie. Ailbhe Malone declared it 'so unthreatening it might have to think twice about holding hands, lest it get overwhelmed'. However, she said this was not 'a bad thing'. She continued: 'Channelling their sterling performance of "My Life Would Suck Without You", "What Makes You Beautiful" is exuberant with a catchy "oh na na na" middle eight. The real genius is that the chord progression is simple enough to be played on an acoustic guitar at a house party.' Harry's band were getting the nod of approval from all corners.

The CBBC *Newsround* website awarded the single four stars out of five, saying: 'Think summer, think sunshine, think parties on the beach with your mates, and you'll get the general vibe of "What Makes You Beautiful". It's classic pop — fun, upbeat and incredibly catchy.' *PopMatters* approved of it too: 'it is a nice get-up-and-go dance number (complete with cowbell!)'.

The commercial response was fairly strong, too. Three weeks ahead of the release date, Sony Music announced that the single had already broken all records for the numbers of pre-orders in the company's history. On release the song debuted at number one in Britain and Ireland — the home nations of the band members. In due course it would perform very well in other territories, too.

The promotional video for the single is a key part of its success – and, by any reasonable judgement, Harry is the star of the show. He and the rest of the band filmed it, directed by director, cinematographer and photographer John Urbano, over two days in Malibu, California. They are seen frolicking on the beach, driving a camper van, playing with a football and much more besides. Their fun is infectious. As he delivers the line about flipping hair in the first chorus, Harry flips his own much-loved curly mane. Here is laid bare the two-way power of the line: the way he flips his hair gets many of his fans overwhelmed.

A gang of girls then join the fun a minute or so in. It is, though, when the band take their tops off to play in the Pacific Ocean that the interest of most viewers will increase. The fact that there are but a few brief scenes of their topless torsos was deliberate. This was less a tease and more a determination on the part of the band's management to take their ages into account and not overly sexualize the band at this early stage of their careers. Noting, for example, the way that Justin Bieber had first conquered the world of pop with a basically squeaky-clean and wholesome image, the management were determined that One Direction should not leap out of their clothes at the first moment as some other boy bands had done. The most intimate moment of the video comes when Harry sings the a cappella part up close and personally to one of the female models.

During a subsequent promotional television interview, Alan Carr had the band in stitches when he asked about a possible dalliance between Harry and a model from their video called Madison. 'Did you take a trip down Madison's avenue?' he asked, much to the band's boyish amusement.

Funnier still was when Carr asked Harry about 'pussygate'. Harry's tongue-in-cheek explanation was pure genius. 'It was completely innocent!' he said. 'Me and Matt had been discussing Christmas presents for our parents and Matt had previously said he wanted to get as many cats as he could for his mum.'

Cowell, pleased with the success his young band was enjoying, took them and Leona Lewis to a fundraising dinner at London's posh Savoy Hotel. Harry turned up in a black suit and bow tie, looking just the part for a gala dinner. At the dinner itself he bid £7,000 for two tickets to the Grand Prix. In another of his cheeky moments, he swiped Niall's bidding card and, without telling his bandmate, slapped an £8,000 bid on a beauty school workshop. Luckily, Niall didn't have to cough up because his bid was bettered by someone else.

Within a matter of days, they were out at another flashy event – this time the GQ Men of the Year awards at London's Royal Opera House. Wearing a Lanvin suit and bow tie, Harry looked spectacular as he rubbed shoulders with the likes of Kylie Minogue, Kelly Brook, Emma Watson and members of the girl group The Saturdays. The band had certainly taken a step up in the style stakes since the early days of The X Factor. This was a hint of things to come for Harry's fashion sensibilities.

For Harry, the most exciting part of the evening came when he saw Bill Nighy, the veteran actor. Harry thought Nighy looked 'sick' – meaning good. He shared a table with James Corden and Nick Grimshaw – both men with whom Harry would form a strong and lasting bond. His way of networking with the rich and famous started immediately. In the years ahead, this knack would quickly make him a highly connected celebrity.

* * *

This is not to say that these early days of fame were always easy for him. There were stumbles along the way. Appearing on Chatty Man had been an amusing experience for Harry. He was relaxed and his wit and charm meant he had oozed star appeal. He had the opposite experience when the band performed their single on the Cowell-created game show *Red Or Black?*. For the first two verses and choruses of the song the audience were shown a specially acted VT of the band travelling to the television studio by Underground and being chased down the road by screaming fans. What was meant as a simple gimmick was interpreted by some viewers as evidence that the band were being shielded from giving a full performance due to a supposed lack of talent when it came to live performance.

However, the rest of the song was sung live in the studio – and it was here where things went wrong. When Harry sang the a cappella section live, his nerves – and breathlessness, having danced around onstage – were both painfully clear. His hands shook as he sang and his eyes looked more than a little anxious. Harry was singing more or less in tune, but the timing was a little off and his breathing was out of sync with the song. He pulled it back and found some composure – had he got the timing wrong the whole performance would have become an embarrassing flop. When he completed the a cappella part successfully he breathed a sigh of relief. Niall patted him on the shoulder and the band launched back into the full crashing chorus.

But after they came off air, Harry's world came crashing down. He remembered how he 'felt a little sorry for himself' over the way he had let his nerves be seen during the a cappella section. But then he logged on to Twitter and searched to see what was being said about him online. During a subsequent documentary interview, he remembered the extent of the abuse that he found, his emotions bubbled over and he struggled to speak. 'I just read, like … so I read … kind of, just a massive list of these comments,' he said. He was devastated. Louis tried to comfort him but realized there was not much he could do. 'I felt powerless,' said Louis later. As Harry scrolled through the abuse that was being spouted about him on

Twitter he realized that, though he wished it were otherwise, he was sensitive to how people perceived him. 'I can take criticism,' he has said. But he adds that if someone writes that they do not like him, he wants to know why, so he found it hard to understand why people were saying these things about him online. He has said since that he has sometimes found it hard not to search for the negativity that he knows exists online. 'I'm very aware that if you go on social media, and look, you can find whatever you're looking for,' he said. 'If you're looking for bad comments, you're going to find bad comments. But people still do it. It's like this weird self-torture.

'I used to do it when I started. Now I don't any more, and I feel this noticeable change in how happy I am, which is nice. But I'm not bashing social media. I think social media also does a lot of good and it's important to notice that and grow with it.'

Meanwhile, he had to deal with his first tabloid storm about a romantic relationship and the downside of social media would loom large in the

> **His liaison with Flack would bring lots of fun and joy to both of them but it would also cause unhappiness, grief and scrutiny.**

episode. Through it, he would learn a great deal about the nature of fame – and also just how vociferous his fan base was. It all started when he met the broadcaster Caroline Flack. His liaison with Flack would bring lots of fun and joy to both of them but it would also cause unhappiness, grief and scrutiny. For Flack, that scrutiny would be a precursor to harsher media examinations in later years. Ultimately, this would all end up with tragedy.

★ ★ ★

Born in November 1979, Flack began her career as an actress, appearing in *Bo' Selecta!* in 2002, and then went on to become a presenter. She appeared in various ITV2 spin-off shows such as *I'm a Celebrity … Get Me Out of Here! NOW!* and *The Xtra Factor*. When the reality show *Love Island* was relaunched in 2015, she was chosen as host and helped make it one of the biggest shows on British TV.

She also made her West End stage debut as Roxie Hart in *Chicago* in 2018, and appeared in a touring version of *Crazy For You*. In her 2015 autobiography *Storm in a C Cup*, she said she and Prince Harry once 'spent the evening chatting and laughing', but as soon as the story 'got out, that was it. We had to stop seeing each other.'

Along the way, the glamorous host had become quite a pin-up for many viewers, including Harry. During these shows, he had noticed her and taken a shine. In an interview he said: 'If Caroline Flack is reading this, say "Hi" from me. She is gorgeous!' In a separate interview, he said he would 'love to take Caroline out' and joked that a date at McDonald's might be an option for them.

Then, at an *X Factor* after-show party at the W Hotel in London in October 2011, they finally met. According to eyewitnesses, he made a beeline for Flack, chatted to her for a while and then put it all on the line by going in for a kiss. They left together in a cab but it is believed that nothing more happened that particular evening. However, he did take to Twitter that night, writing: 'Sometimes things happen and you suddenly get a whole new outlook on life.'

The following morning, Flack tweeted that she had woken 'with the sorest throat and huge glands' and Harry then tweeted that he had woken up 'with man flu and a sore throat'. When Tomlinson subsequently said that Harry 'had found the one,' people began to put two and two together.

The first time they were spotted together it was at the Asia de Cuba restaurant in the St Martin's Lane Hotel in the West End of London. A very fancy eaterie – McDonald's it was not. They reportedly left together in a chauffeured car. But as their relationship began to become public knowledge, it was quickly obvious that many One Direction fans were far from happy at the news.

'I want to kill you, Caroline Flack. Harry is mine, bitch,' read a typical message. Another fan wrote that if Flack were to flirt with Harry, 'I will personally hunt her down and shoot her.' There were many similar messages. Harry and Flack were both shocked by the severity of these social media outbursts. She took to Twitter herself and wrote: 'I'm close friends with Harry. He's one of the nicest people I know. I don't deserve threats.'

Harry said: 'We're good mates and we hang out a lot; we just get on really well so we're friends – we'll see what happens.' He told her not to listen to Twitter, prompting Flack to reflect that: 'He became the mature one at that point!' He would later comment that he thought that 'people should think more before they tweet stuff'.

An ex-boyfriend of Flack's was reportedly also less than pleased with the news of the relationship as he had been hoping for a reconciliation. The man, called Dave Danger, had been a drummer with the indie band The Holloways. In the weeks before she was linked to Harry, she had reportedly been moving closer to him. But then, says a source, she 'left him hanging'. He would not be the last man to be portrayed in the press as angry with Harry for this sort of reason.

When Harry was photographed arriving at Flack's house in the evening and then leaving the following morning, looking tired, the story only rocketed. Later, she was snapped leaving his house and then waving him off for a tour. When she turned up to a One Direction concert she couldn't have failed to spot that there was a huge fan banner bearing the message: 'Flack off, Caroline.' There was a stallholder selling whistles and telling fans to 'whistle if you hate Caroline Flack'. It had been quite an experience for Flack. At thirty-one years of age, she had gone through a fair number of odd times as a result of her fame. She knew better than most that being a famous face brought problems as well as benefits. She also knew that social media could be a lively and unpleasant place, particularly for famous people who, inadvertently or otherwise, got on the wrong side of a large fan base.

But still, the ferocity of the backlash took her by surprise. Harry taking a fancy to her did not, though. 'I already knew that he had a crush on me, he's made it pretty obvious as he's said it in magazines and said it to friends,' she told the *Sun on Sunday*.

Once their relationship became public knowledge, she was widely attacked in the press, with the *Daily Mail* describing her as predatory and saying Harry was 'still a child'. Then Rebecca Ferguson joined the chorus of condemnation, saying: 'I think there's something not right about Caroline and Harry's relationship.' (This, despite the fact that she had herself dated Harry's bandmate Zayn Malik when he was just a teenager himself.)

> Once their relationship became public knowledge, she was widely attacked in the press, with the *Daily Mail* describing her as predatory and saying Harry was 'still a child'.

It seemed a lot of people had things to say about a simple relationship in which no one was harmed. As for Harry's parents, they had mixed feelings about the fling. Des said he thought the age gap was 'a bit extreme' and therefore the relationship was 'ridiculous'. However, Anne said she had 'never really thought it would be a problem'. She added that 'personality is more important than anything else' and reminded us that her husband was 'ten years older than me and it didn't bother me one way or another'.

In any case, the relationship came apart in early 2012. A source told the *Daily Mail* that with such pressures on the band, Harry was 'being realistic about the whole thing'. They added that Harry was 'young' and 'just not ready for a long-distance relationship'. As this was interpreted as Harry 'dumping' Flack, he tweeted a clarification. 'Please know I didn't "dump" Caroline,' he wrote. 'This was a mutual decision. She is one of the kindest, sweetest people I know. Please respect that.' He stayed in touch with her and

'Please know I didn't "dump" Caroline,' he wrote. 'This was a mutual decision. She is one of the kindest, sweetest people I know. Please respect that.'

even more than a year after the break-up, he would send her raunchy text messages bursting with saucy compliments and innuendoes. Or just straightforward boosters. 'You're looking hot,' said one. 'Dirty Harry's at it again,' Flack would joke to friends as his latest missive arrived on her phone.

She said that though she felt she shouldn't have to worry about such an age gap, she accepted that 'some people aren't accepting' of them. Speaking to Now magazine, she added: 'I keep thinking: what have I done wrong?' Turning to the death threats, she said: 'It went too far. It's a form of bullying from people who are hiding behind a computer.' Luckily, she had support from those closest to her. Caroline's friend Dawn Porter wrote: 'To anyone who sent [Flack] nasty or aggressive messages yesterday, I would like to say this, you are repulsive. Chin up, girl x.'

As for the age difference between her and Harry, Caroline said it wasn't a particular issue for her. 'I've never felt I was much older than Harry. I still feel eighteen and I probably act that way half the time.' That said, she admitted that they had tried to keep it all secret at first. 'Although it was just a bit of fun we decided it was best to keep it to ourselves as we were both working for Simon Cowell,' she said.

'We were both single, we got on well and we had a laugh. It was only when it became public knowledge that things turned sour. At the beginning it was all very playful. He joked about being attracted to older women.

'It began to go wrong when he was pictured coming out of my house one morning. And that was that. People started shouting "paedophile" at me in the street, and "pervert".' Speaking some years later, she added: 'I'm not going to ever apologize for it because there was nothing at the time that was serious or bad and nobody was getting hurt.'

More serious trouble came her way when she was charged with assaulting her partner in 2019. Though he did not support the prosecution, the authorities pressed on with it. She quit *Love Island* and then it was announced the case would be going to trial. In February 2020, she was found dead in her London flat. A lawyer for the family said the star had taken her own life.

The family said in a statement: 'We can confirm that our Caroline passed away today, the 15th of February. We would ask that the press respect the privacy of the family at this difficult time and we would ask they make no attempt to contact us and/ or photograph us.' The news shook the world of showbusiness and one can only imagine how it affected Harry, who had yet to comment on the tragedy as this book was completed.

However, his mother Anne shared this touching poem after news broke of Flack's death:

★

How lonely must you feel
To think that must be done
To feel there is no love
To support you through

★

How must your heart ache
To feel so all alone
The public face; the private face
Both vulnerable

★

The mask we all wear
Outside where skies are open
In view of others eyes
Opinions words and cruelty

★

Unmasked and alone
Black hole surrounds
No shoulder or heart
Enough to take the pain away.

★

Just days later, Harry was booked in to perform at the BRIT Awards. He arrived at the ceremony wearing a black ribbon of remembrance on his Gucci suit. During the evening, he sang his solo song 'Falling'. It was an emotional performance. Harry stood in pouring water in a white suit as he performed the powerful ballad. He seemed to have tears in his eyes as he completed the song, perhaps with Flack in his mind. Later in the evening, he wore a different outfit, which included a lapel badge reading: 'Treat People With Kindness'. This was interpreted as a reference to one of Flack's final Instagram posts, which read: 'In a world where you can be anything … Be kind.'

Flack would not be the final older girlfriend he would have and there might be familial reasons why he and his 1D bandmates are so comfortable with older women. Between them, several members of One Direction have many older sisters: Harry has Gemma, Liam has two older sisters, Zayn has three and Louis has four half-sisters. However, Harry argues that his image as a Lothario misrepresents how he sees women of any age. 'A lot of the time, the way it's portrayed is that I only see women in a sexual way. I grew up with just my mum and sister, so I respect women a lot,' he says.

He did little to dispel the perception that he was only interested in older women when he subsequently hinted he had a thing for thirty-something socialite Kim Kardashian. During an interview in America he held up a poster of the curvy celebrity. Attached to it was a Post-it note on which he had scribbled: 'Call me … Maybe?' Then, during a television interview, Zayn teased Harry about his perceived penchant. 'He likes an older woman,' said Zayn, to Harry's palpable discomfort. 'What's your rule? Anyone younger than …' It was then that Harry stepped in to stop Zayn going any further. His humour on the issue was starting to wear thin.

He also points out that the media is quick to leap to conclusions if a reporter or photographer spots him with a girl. 'Quite a lot of the girls I get photographed with are just friends and then, according to the papers, I have, like, 7,000 girlfriends.'

His experience of the negative side of Twitter during the Flack relationship and after the *Red Or Black?* appearance was interesting because One Direction would be the first band to truly harness the power of the social network. Harry was only too aware of the scale of that power.

'It's really important that we connect directly with our fans through the likes of Twitter so they can get to know us,' he told the *Guardian*. 'There'd be no point someone in the office doing it because that would defeat the object. We kept in contact with them and gave them something to look forward to. If it wasn't us on the thing, the fans wouldn't know us.'

However, one woman who was linked with Harry faced so

much abuse from his fans that she felt unable to continue with Twitter. While the band was in New Zealand, he reportedly began dating American model Emma Ostilly. He was said to have taken her on a date, smooched on her doorstep and smuggled her into the band's hotel. 'They really seemed to have a connection and only had eyes for each other,' an onlooker was quoted as saying. The suspiciously familiar vocabulary – used in endless quotes from unnamed 'sources' – brought the veracity of this into question. After Harry explained that she was 'just a friend', Liam backed up his bandmate, saying: 'She's not his girlfriend either.' This was not enough to save her from some fans' venom. She deleted her Twitter account after tiring of the harassment.

We will cover Harry's love life in more detail later, but it is worth remembering the approach of other boy bands to understand how One Direction stood out in regard to their relationships with women. In days gone by, boy-band members were often banned by their management from having girlfriends, or at least publicly admitting as much. Take That, for instance, were ordered not to have girlfriends by their management team as it was feared that they would lose appeal to their fans if they were not perceived as being 'available' romantically.

For One Direction, a decision was made early on that a different approach would be taken. They would be allowed to have girlfriends and to be open about this. At one early meeting with their management the boys were even encouraged to date slightly older women, as it was felt the 'fallout' following a split would be less damaging that way, as a more mature woman would be less likely to kick up a fuss when things went wrong.

As for Harry, he had learned many lessons. About lust, love, the mainstream media and social media. 'Today there are so many more ways for us to be engaged,' he said. 'I think that's the main positive of social media, but there's also a lot that I find super dangerous about social media.

'On a personal level, I feel a noticeable change in how happy I am when I'm not on social media. Someone once described it to me like a house party, where there are three people who are great and twenty-three people who aren't that nice. You just wouldn't go to that party, would you? That kind of summarizes my feelings about social media. I dip in. I see the friends I want to see and I dip out.' It sounds like a wise approach.

* * *

Meanwhile, it was time for the band's debut album to be released. The day that Harry had dreamed of for so long had finally arrived. He and the band had worked hard on it. To bring the album to fruition, the band had worked with a string of impressive names. Wayne Hector, the man who wrote Westlife's mega-hit 'Flying Without Wings', was one of them. Another was Steve Robson, who had worked with James Morrison and Busted. Perhaps the two people they worked with who most excited the boys were RedOne, who has co-produced a string of hits for Lady Gaga, and Ed Sheeran, the ginger-haired singer-songwriter sensation. Harry said that the people they worked with on the album were 'legendary'. There were twenty-two songwriters involved in the tracks on the album. On top of this, the band members themselves get co-writing credits on three of the album's tracks.

Titled *Up All Night*, One Direction's debut album proved to be a carefully selected, brilliantly produced piece of work. 'We worked really hard on the first album to find the right songs,' Harry said. 'They needed to be perfect.' Recording had taken place in three countries: Sweden, the USA and the UK.

The album begins with the band's first hit, 'What Makes You Beautiful'. Everything that made the song great also made it ideal as an album opener. It grabs the attention of the listener right from the opening riff.

In an album with several surprises and changes of pace, the first occurs with track two; in contrast to the opener, 'It's Gotta Be You' is a classic boy-band ballad. The energy is dialled down and the playfulness of 'What Makes You Beautiful' has been replaced by a yearning. Here, the lyrics are full of regret for hurt that has been unintentionally caused to a girl. Who cannot relate to the expressed wish that time could be rewound? The chorus tells the girl that there is no one but her. Gorgeous strings turn this into an epic affair that moves and delights the listener.

Track three sees the sound return to the impish, pop-rock atmosphere of the opener. 'One Thing' is the natural sibling to 'What Makes You Beautiful'. It includes the memorable lyric, 'Shot me out of the sky – you're my kryptonite'. This lyric, which implicitly positions the boys as Superman, is marvellous fun, as is the song itself. This is perfectly weighted pop rock.

The track features some astonishing falsetto vocals, which show the range of the band and add true gravitas to the experience.

Then, the mood changes again. 'More Than This' is the slowest, and most gentle, track on the album. The lyrics about dying inside when they see the girl lie down with another guy hit hard. The track features some astonishing falsetto vocals, which show the range of the band and add true gravitas to the experience. The synthesizer in the chorus is also a feature that brings weight to the track.

The fifth song is a more natural progression from its predecessor. It is the album's title tune. Set to a track reminiscent of early Busted material, it is a fun tale of a riotous teenage party, with its shaking floor, people 'going all the way', broken tables, Katy Perry on the sound system – it is a vivid call to arms to a party generation. Where previous tracks tiptoed or tapped, this one is a stomper.

'I Wish' is a mid-tempo sound very much in the 'album track' category: there is nothing wrong with it, but it does not leap out at the listener. Perhaps it is a little too generic; it certainly seems overly negative in its depiction of romantic jealousy.

It feels like 'Tell Me a Lie' is one of the songs that was written with an American audience in mind: if ever a song on the album was made to be listened to with the roof down on a US freeway, this is it. Its central conceit – that ignorance can sometimes be bliss when it comes to relationships – offered a new perspective to many of the young fans who listened to it.

'Taken' is, in contrast, one to be sung around a bonfire, complete with acoustic guitars. Harry has arguably never sounded better than he does on this track, in which the boys are defiant rather than doting: 'Who do you think you are?' they ask, a hint of menace in their voices. As the music industry journal *Billboard* commented: 'Now the narrator is fending off a bewitching girl trying to break up his current relationship.'

If the next song, 'I Want', reminds you of a mid-career track by McFly, that is for good reason – their chief songwriter and lead singer Tom Fletcher wrote it. Despite making some less than flattering remarks about One Direction when they first came to the public eye, Fletcher quickly noted their commercial potential and happily handed them this song. Some older listeners said the track reminded them of the 1980s hit 'Tainted Love' by Soft Cell, but this wouldn't have meant much to the band's core fan base.

'Everything About You' is far more electro and mainstream pop in sound. Some strong lyrics lift it out of the pack, again underscoring the attention that has gone into the entire affair. *Billboard* said 'the bubblegum verses offer more personality than the standard harmonic hook'. 'Same Mistakes' is a sweet, rolling ballad with a rich backing and a solid vocal performance.

We're at the penultimate track, in which the band say they want to save a girl from her current lot in life. 'Save You Tonight', a song that could easily be performed by JLS or The Wanted, pushes multiple buttons. Few fans would be able to resist such salvation from the lads. *Billboard* said the song was 'enjoyably retro in sound and arrangement'.

For a moment, 'Stole My Heart' sounds like it's going to be a cover of Taio Cruz's 'Dynamite'. But then, during the bridge, the song momentarily reminds the listener of Rihanna's 'Only Girl (In The World)'. An impressive anthem about an impressive-sounding girl brings to a close an impressive album. Perhaps the most pertinent fact of all is that Harry has the most solo vocal time on the album – with around seven minutes of it devoted to him singing alone. Liam comes second, with six minutes of solo time.

★ ★ ★

The album debuted at number two in the UK charts. Impressive in itself, and things got more impressive still when it became the fastest-selling debut album in the UK Albums Chart of 2011. It also reached the top 10 in other countries including Sweden, Ireland, the Netherlands, New Zealand and Australia (it was set for release in America in March 2012). The *Sun*'s face of showbiz Gordon Smart declared: '*Up All Night* will be lapped up by their young fan base' and praised it for its blend of sounds and styles. *Cosmopolitan* magazine felt that the album was full of 'toe-tappers that are just impossible to dislike'; the *Independent* newspaper said the album would 'sell by the zillion'; while the *Daily Star* said it was full of 'belting fun pop anthems'. Having watched the album spring out of the traps both critically and commercially, Harry prepared to join the rest of the band on their first headline tour. Beginning in the middle of December in Watford, they played in cities across the UK and Ireland to fans who had snapped up all the tickets to the shows within minutes of them going on sale – the tour was completely sold out. As well as singing tracks from their album and the B-side 'Na Na Na', they also performed some covers. Among these were 'I Gotta Feeling', by the Black Eyed Peas, the Zutons track 'Valerie', which was made famous by Amy Winehouse, and 'Use Somebody' by Kings of Leon. There were also 'snowball' fights with the plastic snowballs that were sent down from on high during one point in the set, followed later on by silver streamers. With Niall plucking his acoustic guitar for parts of the set and the band indulging in ample between-track banter that the boys had perfected on the *X Factor* tour, the shows made for superb nights out.

Although three of the band, who were inside the bus at the time, suffered temporary head and neck pains, as well as shock, there were no serious injuries.

Naturally, the other ingredient of the experience was the screams of the fans who had been lucky enough to get tickets. Even seasoned concert-goers and staff at the venues were taken aback by the volume of the noise. The only downside of the tour came when their tour bus was smashed into by a car in early January. Although three of the band, who were inside the bus at the time, suffered temporary head and neck pains, as well as shock, there were no serious injuries.

As the tour rolled on, reviews of the debut album continued to be published. For Harry, this was a new style of verdict. Having faced the criticisms of *X Factor* judges on television, he was now facing those of album reviewers in print and online. The latter camp can be every bit as vicious as Cowell and company. However, Robert Copsey of *Digital Spy* said: 'The overall result is an adorable as expected debut that also has a surprising amount of bite. Future boy bands beware: this one means serious business.'

An amusing review came from Zachary Hole of *PopMatters*, who began by listing a series of strikes against Harry's band. It felt he was leading to a demolition of the album but instead he described it as 'a little bit of a revelation when it comes to tweenybopper bubblegum pop'. He continued: 'I don't know how to put this politely, so let's just say that the album, in all of its disposable and of-the-moment glory, doesn't suck. Really. It doesn't suck. In fact, it's actually quite appealing and surprisingly muscular.' He concluded: '*Up All Night* is a well-crafted slice of pop you can pop bubbles to, one that shows that there might be only one place where One Direction can go from here … and that direction would be, admittedly, up.'

Jason Lipshutz noted in *Billboard* that the brilliance of the album's first three songs made it 'feel a bit top-heavy'. However, he said that even on the weakest tracks it 'demonstrates an originality in sound that was necessary for the revitalization of the boy band movement'. Jody Rosen of *Rolling Stone* was less complimentary when he wrote: 'whereas Justin Bieber has charm, that telltale scratchy vocal tone and actual charisma, One Direction are simply five pretty guys with a few decent songs and not much personality'. Rosen concluded: 'Call them One Dimension.'

Simon Price of the *Independent* began his review describing One Direction as a 'cobbled-together quintet of barely pubescent boys'. It sounded like he wasn't an admirer and, sure enough, he said of *Up All Night* that it 'consists of fifteen instalments of inoffensive daytime radio pop'. Adam Markovitz of *Entertainment Weekly* was also rather tough. He said: 'Music groups don't come with much less street cred than this: After failing individually in auditions for the UK's *X Factor* in 2010, five teen crooners were slapped together by judge Simon Cowell into an insta-band.' He said the material 'won't help the group earn much respect in music circles'.

A pure pop album like this was always going to divide the serious music critics, but let's conclude with a positive note. *Cosmo* said the album saw 'Harry and pals' deliver a collection that was 'full of toe-tappers and just IMPOSSIBLE to dislike (so don't even try) it's a thumbs up from us'. It showed, concluded writer Sophie Goddard, that 'there's only One Direction'.

$$\star \quad \star \quad \star$$

Life for Harry and the band was moving fast. Nobody in the band or associated with them wanted to let their moment pass. The prospect of becoming a one-minute wonder, who would disappear as fast as they had appeared, haunted Harry. He wanted to be in the music industry for the long haul and to make his success a truly global thing.

Having formed in 2010 and then released a single and album in 2011, One Direction wanted to up their game in 2012. They were not even content to merely replicate the fun and success of 2011 – they wanted to soar ever higher and better it.

Soon, they would be trying to crack the US market. But first it was time for Britain's most prestigious music awards night – the BRITs. For Harry, it proved to be quite a night. Held at the O2 Arena in February for the second successive year, it was hosted by his new friend James Corden. The band was nominated in the Best British Single category. Given how many successful acts never win a BRIT Award during their career, it was highly significant that One Direction were already on the brink of winning their first. For their category, a public vote had been held to decide the winner. It was listeners to the Capital FM radio station who had voted, but in the excitement of winning the award, Harry thanked the listeners of Radio 1 by accident.

He said: 'And a massive thank you to Radio 1.' Mindful of the enormous damage this could cause One Direction's chances of airtime on Capital, the band's PR firm issued a swift statement via Twitter. 'One Direction forgot to thank the Capital Radio listeners last night when picking up their BRIT Award for "Best British Single",' read the statement. 'This was an oversight as the boys were caught up in the excitement of winning. The band would like to take this opportunity to thank Capital Radio and all their listeners for their support and for voting for them.'

Although Harry was kicking himself over his slip-up, he and his bandmates tried hard not to let it get in the way of some serious celebrating. Later in the night they certainly appeared worse for wear. During an interview, Niall was flushed and Harry slurred and mumbled. When they reappeared for an even later interview, Harry said nothing but merely pointed at the camera in a rather vacant way.

Asked how they would divide the single trophy between them, they joked they would either cut it into pieces or photocopy it. Later, Harry finally admitted that he did make the 'pussygate' comment. With his hard partying perhaps contributing to his mood of candour, he tweeted: 'I admit … I did say "Think how much pussy you're going to get". I apologize.' There were a few sore heads the next morning as they dissected what had been an eventful night for them all, and Harry in particular.

They had to shrug it all off and keep moving … this time in the direction of the USA. They quickly cracked the all-important and almost impossible American market. When you consider the list of top British and Irish acts that have failed to replicate their success Stateside, it becomes clear how hard it is to get it right. Among those who struggled there are Westlife, Robbie Williams and Oasis. Busted, then Britain's biggest pop band and an act huge in Japan, even made an MTV series – called *America Or Busted* – documenting their inability to make it in America. With bands who had ruled the British charts for years failing in America, who would have held out hope for One Direction there?

✳ ✳ ✳

However, more or less immediately after they arrived in America for the big push, Harry and the guys found that they had a huge, fanatical and vocal following there – social media meant that fans already knew about them. They were mobbed in Boston and, when they moved on to Toronto in Canada, a crowd so huge and excitable surrounded their hotel that the police were called. One American media man, from *Billboard*, said: 'There's a lot of possibility here, there's a lot of upside … that level of talent with those kinds of looks … it's really a perfect storm for a massive, massive successful phenomenon.' Given how hard to impress the US media can be, these were very promising words.

The promise turned into reality when their debut single, 'What Makes You Beautiful', first charted in America at number 28 – the highest *Billboard* Hot 100 debut for a UK act for fourteen years. This was exciting enough itself, but even better news was just around the corner.

One Direction became the first UK pop group to debut at number one on the US *Billboard* chart with their album *Up All Night*. They were stunned and humbled by the news. 'We simply cannot believe that we are number one in America,' said Harry. 'It's beyond a dream come true for us. We want to thank each and every one of our fans in the US who bought our album and we would also like to thank the American public for being so supportive of us.'

In a mind-boggling turn of events, comparisons were soon being made between the band and Britain's biggest ever musical export. Not only did One Direction get a slot on *Today*, the biggest breakfast television show in America, they were trailed on the show not as some bunch of outsiders from Britain, but as a band akin to the Beatles. 'Now at 8.39 a.m., with the group that some people are saying are inspiring the next case of Beatlemania …' says the presenter, 'odds are if you do have a teenager in your house, a pre-teen girl, she's already obsessed with One Direction.'

After their imperiousness in the USA, it was time for them to fly to Australia and New Zealand. The hysteria of the fans was shocking there, too. One fan even said she would be willing to be shot by a stun gun to get close to her heart-throbs. 'I'll do anything to see them, I'd even get tasered for this,' she said. 'I don't care, I just have to see them.' The band made such an impact Down Under that when tickets for their eighteen shows there went on sale in September 2013, all 190,000 tickets were instantly snapped up. Country by country, One Direction were conquering the world.

* * *

In November 2012, the band's second album was released, less than a year after their debut offering. *Take Me Home* was beaten out of the traps by the anthemic single 'Live While We're Young'. It proved to be a controversial release, as many critics felt that the lyrics were inappropriately rude for the age group that Harry and co were courting. With its loud guitars, this first track sets a strong tone for the album. It's clear immediately that this collection is going to have a harder, louder sound to it. Co-produced by Carl Falk, the Swedish producer behind 'What Makes You Beautiful', it takes that song and puts it up a gear. Next up comes 'Kiss You', an uptempo catchy and cheeky tune, followed by 'Little Things', which was written by Ed Sheeran, in which things get slower and more serious. 'C'mon, C'mon' takes up the pace again, with a narrative of a boy left high and dry, who then spots a girl in the same dilemma. 'Last First Kiss' is another more serious tune.

Grady Smith of *Entertainment Weekly* said the album was 'not-so-innocent,' while *HitFix*'s Melina Newman said some of the lyrics were 'unwieldy and uncouth' with an 'in between clumsiness that the not-so-little girls will understand'. Given that Harry was the band member most associated with sex, these criticisms seemed aimed more at him than his bandmates. Naturally, none of this bothered the sales – it hit number one in the UK and a raft of other countries.

> He was keen to appeal beyond the band's large but demographically limited fan base. He also wanted to show the range of his vocal ability, rather than being cramped into one style.

Robert Copsey from *Digital Spy* felt the band were not progressing musically any faster than a 'snail's pace'. *Entertainment Weekly*'s Adam Markovitz felt the album was rushed, a collection with 'barely enough zip to keep the kids up past dinner'. Alexis Petridis said the band's fan base would lap it up, but: 'To anyone else, the mystery of One Direction's success – or at least the sheer scale of it – remains as opaque as ever.' The words of the *New York Times*' Jon Caramanica will have hit Harry hard, as the critic felt the band members' vocals were 'fundamentally interchangeable', with only Malik 'breaking free from the pack vocally with any regularity'.

Here we can find the roots of Harry's frustrations with the limitations of the One Direction brand. As is clear from his solo material and the image he has sought in recent years, he was keen to appeal beyond the band's large but demographically limited fan base. He also wanted to show the range of his vocal ability, rather than being cramped into one style.

And to be clear, there were plenty of positive responses to *Take Me Home*. A review on the now-defunct BBC Music website said: 'It works ... the music itself is of a notable quality. Polished and dependable, despite its safety there are some show-stopping pop anthems present, with the instantaneous chorus of "C'mon C'mon" perhaps the best thing 1D have put their name to.' The *Daily Express*'s Simon Gage said, 'the voices are good and the charm undiminished'.

Again, the commercial performance spoke more than anything: globally, *Take Me Home* topped the charts in more than thirty-five countries, and was the fourth bestselling album of 2012, shifting 4.4 million units. With Harry sharing a songwriting credit for 'Back For You', these sales meant something for his bank balance.

Within twelve months, the band released their third album. *Midnight Memories* was heralded by a teaser video of Harry spelling the word 'Mid' out of a pile of alphabet cards on the floor. On this album Harry had a hand in the writing of four tracks: 'Story of My Life', 'Happily', 'Right Now' and 'Something Great'. Despite being released at the year's end, it was the bestselling album worldwide in 2013 with 4 million copies sold globally.

The reaction was generally one of praise – and an observation that the band's sound had become rockier and more mature. Kitty Empire of the *Guardian* said that 'after two albums of flirting, hand-holding and coltish fumbling at parties, One Direction might just have finally gone all the way on their third album'. *USA Today* said: '*Midnight* uses classic rock as a colour the way last year's *Take Me Home* used electronic dance music.' Chris Payne of *Billboard* pointed to the new prominence of the guitar in the material. It was almost inevitable that, as the band approached a rockier sound, someone would object to One Direction's arrival in this territory. The *Independent*'s Andy Gill said it was a 'fumbling transition from pop to rock'. He said the album was 'clumsy' and laced with 'insincerity'. But *Idolator* was more complimentary, calling *Midnight Memories* 'one of the sturdier pop releases in recent memory'.

* * *

For Harry, a particularly pertinent review came in the *Los Angeles Times*. Mikael Wood noted from a recent performance that 'the group has been affecting a studied looseness onstage, as well ... especially Harry Styles, the band's de facto frontman, who'd even adopted Keith Richards' debauched-pirate headscarf look'. Wood went on to note that Harry 'went further on Sunday's American Music Awards, pushing his voice during the new album's "Story of My Life" beyond the usual boy-band precision into a kind of tortured man-bellow. By established One Direction standards, this was basically Eddie Vedder doing Pearl Jam's "Jeremy".' Again, it felt like Harry was standing ahead of the pack.

Which he continued to do on the band's fourth album, which was called, fittingly enough, *Four*. Horan is credited with coming up with the name of the album, although that is not the biggest honour. The album's two singles, 'Steal My Girl' and 'Night Changes', were the standout moments. Significantly, it was the album that saw band members play an even bigger part in the songwriting process. Louis and Liam worked on much of the album with songwriters Julian Bunetta, John Ryan and Jamie Scott. Zayn and Harry also co-wrote tracks with Bunetta, Ryan, Scott and producer Johan Carlsson.

The album was less predictable than its predecessors and so was the critical response. The *Daily Telegraph* said it detected an 'unlikely comparison to Bruce Springsteen' and the *Independent* said of Harry's band that 'they've all but gone the full New Joisey route, with several songs making brazen grabs for that rock heartland territory'.

The *Boston Globe* said the album 'is the first one that doesn't immediately summon memories of *The X Factor*' and that while 'its mix of driving power pop, muscular harmonies, and acoustic alchemy is as manicured as the group's previous bestsellers', it also 'hints at a broader future for the lads'. *Vice* singled out Harry for praise, saying, 'Styles's raspy tone sounds much more at home in this sort of rock sound than it ever did on bubblegum pop'.

Time made a similar point, writing that 'on *Four*, it's easier than ever to pick out the voices of each member, from Tomlinson's sweet, feminine tenor to Malik's muskier, more sensual tone and Styles's raspy swagger'.

Slant magazine said 'the album's irresistibly obvious choruses, hackneyed sentiments, and puppy-eyed earnestness can come off as endearing when the songwriting is clever enough, but every misstep is ... a painful reminder of One Direction's status as a manufactured, focus-grouped pop entity'.

Billboard was not so blown away, either. It said Harry and the band were 'experiencing some growing pains as they attempt to evolve from boys to men – and wind up caught in limbo'. Chuck Arnold continued: 'It's a tricky transition that New Kids on the Block, Backstreet Boys and others never successfully navigated. Welcome to 1D's awkward phase.' Of Harry's track, he remarked, 'its iffy hostage metaphor ... fail(s) to hold you captive'.

> Harry and the band were 'experiencing some growing pains as they attempt to evolve from boys to men – and wind up caught in limbo'.

Again, the response most pertinent to Harry's future came in the *Los Angeles Times*. Mikael Wood said that listening to the Harry of 2012 and the Harry of 2014 made the intervening two years really 'seem like an eternity'. Wood continued that the album was based on the 'same hip reference points as your average Coachella act: Fleetwood Mac, the Beach Boys, David Bowie', concluding that: 'They're growing up not by going wild but – get this – by relaxing. And the result is their best work yet.' These words about One Direction's penultimate album could almost exactly apply to either of Harry's subsequent solo collections.

> The song, co-written by Harry, certainly captured the attention of many people. It was described as 'spunky' and 'ripe with lust and physical expressions of affection'.

Rolling Stone described Harry as a 'weapons-grade hottie' and noted that he got the same vocal duties as 'take-him-or-leave-him Irishman Niall Horan'. It described 'Stockholm Syndrome' as 'the album's brightest song' and 'a slick, body-moving R&B ditty'. It said Harry's lyrics 'could also be read as a meek cry for help from deep within the prison of celebrity (even if it totally isn't)'.

The song, co-written by Harry, certainly captured the attention of many people. It was described as 'spunky' and 'ripe with lust and physical expressions of affection' by *Time*. During promotional interviews, Harry was asked about it frequently. He was playful and outspoken about what inspired him to write the track. He admitted (with what one feature described as a 'shit-eating grin') that 'Stockholm Syndrome' was 'about a nympho'.

Upon its release on 12 November 2014, the album shot to the top of the UK Albums Chart, with 142,000 copies sold during its first week. Based on UK sales, it was certified gold by the BPI (British Phonographic Industry) in its first week, and certified platinum in its fourth week.

Across the pond in the USA, it debuted at number one on the *Billboard* 200 chart in the week ending 23 November 2014, with sales of 387,000. Therefore, Harry's band became the first musical group to have each of their first four studio albums debut at number one.

There are so many facts one can note about *Four* but the most significant is this: it was the final One Direction album in which Zayn Malik played a part. The boy from Bradford and the rest of the band were about to go in two separate directions. After that, the band's days would be numbered. For Harry, this would prove to be the start of something even bigger.

CHAPTER FOUR

WHERE DID IT ALL GO WRONG?

For many pundits, the biggest surprise over the exit of one member of One Direction was that the member in question was not Harry Styles. Ever since the second half of the live shows on *The X Factor*, it had very much seemed like Harry was being marked out of the pack. It was widely felt that, were One Direction to break up, he was the member who had least to lose. Articles speculating that he was about to walk away from the band would appear regularly.

Part of the reason Harry was marked out was based on past pop bands. Once Robbie Williams became the standout star of Take That, everyone assumed he would eventually walk away from the band. In July 1995, those predictions came true when it was announced that Robbie had left, leaving his former bandmates to struggle on without him.

Then came the saga surrounding Charlie Simpson of Busted. The tall, handsome lead singer seemed to outgrow his two bandmates in all senses. This, taken together with his preference for a harder sound than Busted allowed, made it seem inevitable that he would tire of the pop-rock outfit. In November 2015, he told his bandmates he was leaving and the band broke up on the spot.

Once Harry became the most charismatic and starry member of One Direction, pop pundits felt it was just a matter of time until he left to pursue his own interests. In short, the sense was always that Harry was simultaneously the most important member and also the one most likely to cause the band to collapse. So it was ironic that when the band finally began to come apart at the seams, it was not Harry but another member who was responsible.

> Harry was simultaneously the most important member and also the one most likely to cause the band to collapse.

Nevertheless, the demise of the band began when Zayn left in 2015. An official statement told stunned fans that 'after five incredible years Zayn Malik has decided to leave One Direction. Niall, Harry, Liam and Louis will continue as a four-piece and look forward to the forthcoming concerts of their world tour and recording their fifth album, due to be released later this year.'

Zayn himself remarked: 'I know I have four friends for life in Louis, Liam, Harry and Niall. I know they will continue to be the best band in the world.' Commenting on the pop bombshell, his now former bandmates said: 'We're really sad to see Zayn go, but we totally respect his decision and send him all our love for the future. The past five years have been beyond amazing, we've gone through so much together, so we will always be friends. The four of us will now continue.'

These official statements were all anodyne and positive enough. It was only some time after Zayn had left that he began to deliver a more prickly verdict on the band and on Harry in particular. The claws well and truly came out. Speaking to *Fader* magazine, Zayn said One Direction's music was 'generic as f---' and didn't fit his style. 'Whenever I would suggest something, it was like it didn't fit us. There was just a general conception that the management already had what they wanted for the band and I just wasn't convinced with what we were selling,' he complained.

Later, he told *Rolling Stone* that One Direction's material was 'not music I would listen to'. He asked his interviewer: 'Would you listen to One Direction at a party with your girl? I wouldn't. To me, that's not an insult, that's me as a twenty-two-year-old man.' These were admirably truthful words and it was refreshing to hear someone in the pop world say what was on their mind. All the same, for some One Direction fans it was upsetting.

Then, Zayn actually began to put the boot in on Harry himself. For the final months of Zayn's time in the band, there had been rumours that the pair had fallen out. Even so, it was still a surprise when Zayn spoke about Harry in such terms. Turning to his experiences with his former bandmate, Malik said he and Harry were never close. He said he 'never really spoke to Harry' and that he had never been under the impression they would keep in touch after Malik left the band. 'I didn't make any friends from the band,' he told *GQ*. 'It's not something that I'm afraid to say. I definitely have issues trusting people.'

Harry took the high road when he responded to Malik's comments about One Direction's music – he told *Rolling Stone*: 'I think it's a shame he felt that way … but I never wish anything but luck to anyone doing what they love. If you're not enjoying something and need to do something else, you absolutely should do that. I'm glad he's doing what he likes, and good luck to him.'

However, he later had a light-hearted dig at Malik. When he hosted and performed on *Saturday Night Live*, he made a reference to his boy-band days, saying: 'I love those guys, they're my brothers: Niall, Liam, Louis, and, uh, Ringo, yeah, that's it.' This was in reference to Ringo Starr of the Beatles – a much-mocked member of the rock family.

For the band, Malik's exit initially brought them closer together. With the media sensing a scalp and obituaries of the band itself already being written, Harry and the other three remaining members developed something of a bunker mentality. This often happens when any sort of team feels under attack – they develop a tighter, almost defiant, union. It's them against the world.

'One thing that was good is that it made us really bond,' said Harry, speaking of that time. 'It made us look at what we had and really know we wanted to keep it. It also made us really focus on making the best album we could. You go through so much together as a band that no one really understands, but ultimately it just makes you closer.'

> 'You go through so much together as a band that no one really understands, but ultimately it just makes you closer.'

As a four-piece, they put out one more album: *Made In The A.M.* It was preceded by three singles: 'Drag Me Down', released on 31 July 2015; 'Perfect', released on 16 October 2015; and 'History', which came out on 6 November 2015. The middle one of those singles was written by Harry, as he continued to have a hand in composition. He also co-wrote another album track, 'Olivia'. Harry declared the release to be 'the best album we feel we've done'.

The *Daily Telegraph* said that Harry sang with 'jaded weariness' on

'Perfect' but *Billboard* said it was a 'cool synth-pop tune' and *Digital Spy* said it was a 'scintillating slice of 80s pop'. *All Music*'s take on Harry's vocals was the opposite of the *Daily Telegraph*'s: it said the track was 'the album's best radio song, with a nice moody verse and some real emotional punch provided by Harry Styles's vocal on the super-hooky chorus.'

Hollywood Life was even more cheery, with Shira Benozilio declaring it 'one of my favorites on this album – it's such an uplifting love song with great lyrics and a great beat'. *Idolator* pointed out the presumed connection between 'Perfect' and Harry's reported famous ex as a 'subtweet-level dig at Taylor Swift'.

The same review felt that 'Perfect' might be a look ahead. 'It's a song that compositionally sounds a lot like Swift's own "Style", which was about guess who, and basically posits this thesis from Styles himself: if you want a brooding bad boy who treats you like crap for a fling, not a boyfriend, I'm your man. That's about as edgy as the group has ever gotten, and it could possibly be a nod to the kind of persona Styles himself wants to set up in his solo work.' More on Swift, Harry and this song later.

Billboard said the album was 'not a world-changing record, and 50 years from now, people won't study the cover photo to see whether Harry Styles – arguably 1D's dreamiest dreamboat – is sending some secret message with the way he's sitting'. It added that the remaining band members sound 'a little bummed'.

Rolling Stone felt that *Made In The A.M.* was '1D's *Let It Be* – the kind of record the world's biggest pop group makes when it's time to say thanks for the memories'. The other song Harry co-wrote, 'Olivia', also received flattering praise. *Drowned in Sound* said it was 'the only brand new wonder'. Kate Solomon wrote that 'it has everything from alliteration to a Willy Wonka reference that goes nowhere and means nothing. There are Disney flourishes and Beatles-ish backing harmonies and it's been stuck in my head for days. It's the only song on *Made In The A.M.* that sounds even vaguely like anyone is having any fun.'

It was released in November 2015. In the UK, the album debuted at number one and became the fastest-selling album of 2015 at that stage. In the USA the album debuted at number two on the *Billboard* 200, with 459,000 album-equivalent units (402,000 pure album sales), behind Justin Bieber's *Purpose*. It was the band's first album not to debut at number one and though a number two on the US charts is something most pop bands would dream of, the fact they did not top that chart perhaps tells its own story – the band just weren't as enticing without Zayn.

For Harry, the cracks were continuing to show. He even felt in the recording studio that he was outgrowing the band's sound. 'For me, the albums got higher, so they became harder to sing, so I knew if I didn't come off stage and go to bed I wouldn't be able to sing the next night,' he said. 'Also, it's just not for me. I'd rather wake up with a clear head.'

According to some reports, it was Harry who suggested the band go their separate ways and he first floated the idea of a hiatus in 2014 – before Malik left the band. He was beginning to develop bigger ambitions. He was beginning to look at breaking out by himself.

Not every member of the band was delighted with the idea. It's safe to say, for instance, that Louis Tomlinson was not a fan. 'I was f***ing fuming at first,' he told Capital FM. 'I was bitter and angry, I didn't know why we couldn't just carry on. But now, even though I don't fully understand everyone's individual reasons, I respect them.' However, negotiating the end of any band is never going to be an easy process. Navigating the egos and feelings of each member is an almost impossible task to get right. When it's a band as popular and complex as One Direction, the process will obviously be harder. This was not like when Harry wound up his childhood band, White Eskimo.

* * *

ABOVE Harry experiencing new-found fame when greeted by fans at his hometown in Cheshire in 2010.

BELOW With his mum, Anne Twist, who encouraged him to audition for *The X Factor*.

ABOVE One Direction are crowned *The X Factor* winners, 2010: (left-right) Liam Payne, Louis Tomlinson, Harry Styles, Zayn Malik, Niall Horan with Simon Cowell (centre).

BELOW The band sign copies of their new single 'What Makes You Beautiful' at HMV, Oxford St, London, 2011.

LEFT Leaving *The X Factor* studios in Wembley after a live show in the early days of his fame.

ABOVE One Direction collect their specially created Global Success award at The BRITs, The O2 Arena, London, 2013.

BELOW Harry signs autographs while promoting the band's film, *This Is Us*, Japan, 2013.

ABOVE Harry plays Tattoo Roulette on *The Late Late Show with James Corden*, Los Angeles, 2015.

BELOW Harry appearing on NBC's *The Today Show* to celebrate the release of One Direction's new album *Four* at Universal City Walk, Orlando, 2014.

RIGHT Harry and Rita Ora pose for a photo in the VIP area at The O2 and War Child BRIT Awards Concert featuring Muse, London, 2013.

LEFT Taylor Swift and Harry on a night out in New York, 2012.

ABOVE AND BELOW One Direction (minus Zayn) play their final gig at Sheffield Arena before their year-long break, 2015.

Above Displaying some of his many tattoos at the Teen Choice Awards, California, 2013.

That hiatus was officially announced in 2015. In truth, it only confirmed what was already known. With all sorts of speculation floating around, Harry's bandmates tried to clear the air on Twitter. 'Ok so lots of rumours going round,' wrote Horan. 'We are not splitting up, but we will be taking a well-earned break at some point next year.' Tomlinson added: 'Your support is truly indescribable! It's just a break. We're not going anywhere!!' Payne said: 'So glad everything has been cleared up today and ur support with it is amazing not that we

> He had ambitions for the future and wanted more autonomy in his career.

could ever expect anything less your amazing [sic].' He also promised 'so much more to come'.

Harry spoke later about the hiatus and what might happen next for him. He had ambitions for the future and wanted more autonomy in his career. 'I wanted to step up,' he said. 'There were songs I wanted to write and record, and not just have it be "Here's a demo I wrote." Every decision I've made since I was sixteen was made in a democracy. I felt like it was time to make a decision about the future … and maybe I shouldn't rely on others.'

He also was mindful that some bands are so cynical that they wring dry the passion (and purses) of their fan base. Showing once more his respect for his fans, Harry was determined that One Direction would not do this. 'I didn't want to exhaust [the band's] fan base,' he said. 'If you're short-sighted, you can think: "Let's just keep touring," but we all thought too much of the group to let that happen. You realize you're exhausted and you don't want to drain people's belief in you.'

We will examine later whether there is likely to be a reunion, or whether an unofficial split was called a 'hiatus' merely to soften the blow for devastated One Direction fans. Niall Horan said he had told his managers: 'When One Direction comes knocking, fook what I'm doing. I don't give a shit if I sold out arenas or won Grammys. I wouldn't be doing this if it wasn't for that.'

Louis has also been positive about the idea. 'There is no question of if – it's a must,' he insisted on ITV's *Lorraine* show. 'And I think we're all on the same page with that one. It would be too difficult for any of us to say no. It's one of those ones.'

Even Zayn did not rule out a reunion. 'Who knows? … I don't know,' he said, speaking to *The Sunday Times Culture* magazine. 'If the time was right and that was the thing to do, then I would make that decision when it came around.'

Harry is the member who has been more cagey about a reunion. 'I love the band and would never rule anything out in the future,' he has said. However, he has also played down the chances of them getting back together. 'When we started people always asked, "Where do you think you'll be in five years?" It's a difficult question to answer. I would never say we'll never do anything ever again but it's good for us to be exploring different things.

'Maybe at some point everyone will want to do something again but it'll be better if it happens naturally like, "Hey, we all really want to do this again." If that were to happen it would be amazing.

'I would never rule that out. It's the most important, greatest thing that ever happened to me, being in that band. It completely changed my life.'

That said, it is worth returning to the examples of Williams and Simpson we touched upon earlier in this chapter. As Take That and Busted broke up, few people would have given much of a chance to the idea of either member taking part in any form of reunion. Sure enough, when Take That first got back together, there was no sign of Williams. After years of jibes between him and his former bandmate Gary Barlow, it was no surprise that he was not rushing into any reunion.

Likewise, when Busted's James Bourne and Matt Willis took their first tentative steps towards a reunion, in the hybrid super-band

McBusted, Simpson was not part of the collective. Given that he had seemingly burned bridges with his dismissive attitude towards his former band, again, no one was in shock when he sat out McBusted.

Yet ultimately, both men did return. Robbie joined Take That on tours and albums, and when Busted proper got back together, Simpson was there, centre stage, looking happy to be back with his old compadres. So those who cannot imagine Harry ever rejoining One Direction should reflect that the pop world can often surprise you. Certainly, if the price is made right, you'd be surprised how many people backtrack on their previous insistences.

Meanwhile, Harry continues to be prickly towards those who criticize One Direction fans. Far from disowning them, he continues to demand that people respect them. 'I mean, I think the thing is that people stereotype it as their attraction to the music is something other than the music,' he told National Public Radio. 'And I think that's unfair. And honestly, I think it's just writing people off. I think – I mean, it's kind of rude.'

Rumours of an issue between him and Tomlinson have been dismissed. When the band went their separate ways, reports in the *Mirror* and the *Sun* insinuated that there had been a major issue between the two members. They said that in September 2011, Harry and Louis were living as housemates in a rented £3 million north London flat. Then suddenly, claimed the story, at the start of 2012 they stopped talking and moved out. 'Apart from Harry and Louis, no one knows exactly what caused the falling-out – they didn't even tell the other boys the full details,' a source told the *Sun* at the time.

'But it was very serious and their friendship has never recovered. Everyone involved in the band is well aware of the animosity between them. It's been central to everything else that came next with the band because there was suddenly a massive divide.'

The *Mirror* also claimed that Harry 'refused to even travel with Louis and the fallout would become so serious that bosses reportedly had to find a way to make their last three albums without the boys having to spend any time together in the studio.' This story has been denied several times, including by Horan, who told fans not to believe a word of it. 'We stand strong as a band and we're brothers,' he tweeted.

Another source of rumoured tension came after Malik and Tomlinson were filmed smoking what appeared to be cannabis in the back of an SUV on their way to a concert in Peru in 2014. From behind the camera, Tomlinson can be heard saying, 'So here we are, leaving Peru. Joint lit. Happy days!'

It was said that 'straight-laced Harry' was 'furious' about the pair's 'stupid and reckless' antics. 'Harry is annoyed about the whole debacle. This should be one of the biggest weeks of the band's career … Instead it has been taken over by this controversy,' an insider reportedly told the *Sun*. It was claimed, separately, that Payne's partying was so wild that Harry 'refused to go socialize with the band unless good guy Niall was there to keep the peace'. These claims have never been verified by Harry or anyone else in the band.

Nevertheless, after some of Malik's remarks – in interview and song – about the One Direction years, Harry's positive and respectful tones will have warmed the hearts of the 1D army. Again, we see the values instilled in him by Anne coming good. His manners make him a class act. Which would not hurt him at all as he left the tunnel-like experience that the band's years had been and emerged blinking into the sunlight of his new existence.

He did not leave the party with a bitter parting shot shouted over his shoulder. Instead, he respected what he had done, and spoke of his excitement. 'The nice thing for me is that I'm not coming away from the band feeling like I wasn't able to do what I wanted to do,' said Harry. 'I loved it and it was what I wanted but I'm enjoying writing at the moment; trying new things.'

CHAPTER FIVE

FREEDOM

When pop bands break up, their members often go off the rails for a while. Paparazzi shots show them falling out of nightclubs as dawn breaks. Unnamed 'eyewitnesses' tell readers that the star was partying hard. After a while, the photographers try to get snaps of the band member looking overweight and dishevelled. The overall media drive is to show that the star is all washed up, with no hope for the future. For Harry, life after One Direction was quite different to this. Rather than falling, he soared.

Rather than becoming a party animal, he became a spiritual being. With this sudden freedom and all the temptation it brings, Harry began to spend more time reflecting on life and its meaning. To what degree he is religious, or spiritual, or simply exploring belief systems, is something he has rarely commented upon. He was asked by US comedienne and broadcaster Chelsea Handler if he was religious. His first response to the question was not an answer, more an expression of awe at the question. He simply said: 'Wow.'

Handler pressed on, though. She continued: 'I mean, you seem kind of spiritual to me, like hippie spiritual. I didn't know if you were religious.' This led Harry to the right path and he seemed calmer. 'I'm glad you said it, I feel like anyone who says "I'm spiritual" sounds a little wanky,' he said. 'But yeah, I definitely consider myself to be more spiritual than religious.'

He went on: 'I'm not super tied into certain rules but I think it's naïve to say nothing exists and there's nothing above us or more powerful than us. I think that's a little narrow-minded. I definitely believe in karma. I think "everything happens for a reason" is a difficult one because there's a lot of shit happening in the world that's so unfair right now. So it's hard to look at that stuff and think, "Well, everything happens for a reason."

'But I definitely think there's something, that it's not just us. It's kind of crazy to think that it's just us. I'm not saying I believe in aliens, but you know what I mean.'

* * *

Harry's dalliances with various faiths and belief systems have been an interesting trend to watch. Chief among them has been his reported interest in the Jewish faith. The *Daily Star* reported in 2014 that Styles had an 'obsession' with Judaism. He had a custom-made 'kippah' skullcap and tweeted ahead of Passover: 'Looking forward to Seder night. Always get a bit nervous when I have to sing Ma'nish Ta'na. But do love a shmorreh matzah. Happy pesach x.'

He had also tweeted about another Jewish festival, Purim. 'Enjoy your seudah today and boo loudly at hamann during the megillah!! x', he wrote. Then, before Yom Kippur, when Jewish people fast, he wrote: 'Eating as much as I can now. Gonna be a tough 25 hours. My problem is I am always hungry straight after kol nidre. Fast well everyone!'

Despite not being Jewish, in 2014 he appeared in the *Jewish Chronicle*'s Power 100 list. The newspaper admitted that Styles 'may not be Jewish but he seems very much at ease with a Jewish lifestyle'. He was seen wearing 'a silver Star of David at the Teen Choice awards, hangs out at kosher eateries and is not afraid to throw the odd Yiddish word or two into the conversation'.

> It has been claimed that Harry was involved with the mystical branch of Judaism, Kabbalah, which has attracted many celebrity followers, most notably Madonna.

Harry's interest in Judaism began when he befriended film director Ben Winston, who has worked on *The X Factor* and who directed the video for 'Story of My Life'. 'I was making a film with One Direction and I'd just moved into my very quiet house in London ... and a young man who I was working with, by the name of Harry Styles, asked me if he could live in our attic for a few weeks,' Winston said at the 2018 Television Critics Association in Los Angeles. Later, a sitcom inspired by this domestic set-up was made, called *Happy Together*. Harry was even an executive producer on the show.

He would often eat with Winston at a kosher restaurant in the north London Jewish district Golders Green. He became so synonymous with the eatery that when it closed down in 2014, the Jewish press rushed to non-Jewish Harry for his thoughts. His spokesman revealed he was 'mortified' at the news. 'London's culinary scene has lost a huge part of its neshama,' he said on behalf of the singer.

The *Daily Star* claimed that Harry was involved with the mystical branch of Judaism, Kabbalah, which has attracted many celebrity followers, most notably Madonna. It even claimed that he was giving up sex as part of the deal. 'Harry is really serious about this,' said an unnamed source. 'He feels he doesn't want to be that guy who is known for bedding celebs any more. He feels it's getting in the way of him having a proper, meaningful relationship and Kabbalah is giving him the discipline to finally quit sex for a sustained period.'

> Later he delved into the east, as he began to practise yoga and meditation.

The red strings of Kabbalah were once a fixture on the wrists of many famous people, including Harry. However, given that Harry has never confirmed an interest in the belief system, let alone spoken of going celibate as part of the deal, it seems that this particular slice of speculation was not accurate.

Later he delved into the east, as he began to practise yoga and meditation. The *Sun* reported that when Harry was in Bangkok he 'travelled for forty minutes on his own to see one temple and embrace his spiritual side'. A source added: 'He's been meditating and doing yoga in Thailand and also spent time wandering around markets to soak up the culture. Harry likes to party too but he thinks it's important to have some balance. It can be seriously stressful being on the road all the time so it's good for him to explore the countries.'

His interest in yoga is certainly a real thing, as he has spoken of it and been spotted practising it. When a fan called Rachel spotted Harry at a yoga class in Los Angeles, she could hardly contain her excitement. Let's be precise: she couldn't contain her excitement. Putting on the Caps Lock key on Twitter, she wrote: 'YOU GUYS YOU GUYS YOU GUYS I WENT TO YOGA TODAY AND HARRY ****ING STYLES WAS THERE IN THE SAME CLASS AND AFTER HE SAID EXCUSE ME TO ME AND WAS RIGHT NEXT TO ME BY THE MAT CLEANING STATION AND YES HE CLEANED HIS

OWN MAT GOD BLESS GOD BLESS HE HAD A BANDANA IN HIS HAIR.'

Wow, imagine how full on she'd be *without* the yoga.

He also got involved with transcendental meditation. Known by some West Coast adherents as 'TM', it is a form of silent mantra meditation, created by Maharishi Mahesh Yogi. Although there is no objectively certified evidence of health benefits from the practice, it is widely accepted that it comes with many, both physical and emotional.

Harry has namechecked the hatha yoga practice known as the sun salutation. This practice, known in Sanskirt as Surya Namaskar, is a graceful sequence of twelve positions performed as one continuous exercise. It is often used as a warm up for full yoga classes, particularly in branches of hatha yoga such as the Sivananda tradition.

This practice became such a big deal for Harry that when he was interviewed by *Rolling Stone* magazine, he jokingly suggested the headline 'Soup, Sex, and Sun Salutations'. From being named as an important Jew, despite not being Jewish, he was now coming across as more of an Eastern yogi.

What with all these jokes, unnamed sources and speculation, it might be best to rely on Harry's words. Writing on Twitter, he once answered a fan's question about this very topic, saying: 'I'm christened but not really that religious ... is that ok?' For a non-religious man from a Christian background, he had sure delved into some very religious areas. The space that life after One Direction afforded him helped Harry to become clearer on his spiritual journey. He wears a crucifix and has been seen crossing himself as he walks onstage for performances. So perhaps this space is one worth watching.

* * *

When it came time to start releasing his solo material, Harry suddenly felt both excited and exposed. 'I think I've never felt this vulnerable putting out music because I just don't think it's a piece of myself that I've ever really put out there before,' he told National Public Radio.

'And just simple fact – when there's other people around you, you share the good stuff, but you also get to share the bad stuff and kind of hide behind everyone else a little bit. So with this, yeah, it is scary. But I think it was time for me to kind of be scared, I guess.'

If Harry was excited then so was the world. Since the first whispers of a solo career in 2015, the pop world had been waiting for Harry's own material. From early on in One Direction, it was Harry who stood out for many as the band member with the best chance of a successful solo career. It was widely felt that he had the highest reserves of the necessary qualities: a strong voice, huge charisma, sex appeal and an element of mystique.

So the longer 2015 wore on, the more excited people got about the prospects of Harry's plans. Fans and journalists alike became online sleuths, searching the internet for clues as to what was on the cards. At the end of that year, it was discovered that four new song titles had been logged for Harry on the songwriter registrations list. The titles were: '5378 Miles', 'Already Home', 'Coco' and 'Endlessly'.

Things started to happen fast. In January 2016, a source close to One Direction said that the hiatus had turned into a split. 'The 1D thing just ran its course,' he said. 'They'll remain friends, but they are exhausted and want solo careers.' However, representatives for

> 'I think I've never felt this vulnerable putting out music because I just don't think it's a piece of myself that I've ever really put out there before.'

the band denied the report, telling *Billboard*: 'Nothing has changed regarding hiatus plans for the group, and all will be revealed in due time from the band members' own mouths.'

Next, in February 2016, Harry signed a recording contract with Columbia Records, the label behind One Direction. Then, following in the footsteps of superstars such as Beyoncé, he set up his own record company. The listing for 'Sign of the Times' immediately made this clear, with its accreditation to Erskine Records Ltd under exclusive licence to Columbia Records.

It was also discovered that Harry had become a company director. He is a director of companies including HSA Publishing Ltd (founded 2014) and Rollcall Touring Ltd (founded 2012). This might seem a dreary detail but it put him in a more powerful position than many pop stars. As *Music Business Worldwide* put it: 'Smart boy, that one.'

Meanwhile, a new team was being assembled around him. His manager was Jeffrey Azoff. He is the son of industry legend Irving Azoff. His father is a former CEO of Live Nation and Ticketmaster, who has also represented acts such as Christina Aguilera, Thirty Seconds To Mars and Bon Jovi. In 2012 he was named *Billboard*'s most powerful man in music. So Harry was in good hands. As *Hollywood Reporter* put it: 'The name Azoff is synonymous with power.' Father and son have much in common. The same publication says Jeffrey is 'the spitting image of the mogul in his younger days'.

Speaking to *Billboard* in 2019, when he was thirty-three years of age, Jeffrey quipped that his experience in the industry goes back twenty-two years: 'When the guy who coaches your soccer games is always on the phone making deals in the music business, you have the ability at a young age to sound like you know what you're talking about, even if you might not.' He has previously worked with a galaxy of stars, including Britney Spears, Avril Lavigne, the Eagles and Mac Miller.

Despite the advantages that his background has brought him,

Azoff insists that the record industry is one in which anyone can succeed, in spite of their past and family. 'If you're anyone with an idea and some talent, whether you're an artist or you're in the business, you can have a successful career in the music business,' he said.

'The great thing about Harry is, he has so many ideas and he's the type of artist who knows exactly who he is.'

Azoff says that from the start of their relationship, he and Harry made a deal that they would make everything about having fun, then the music would follow. 'Most of the time, it doesn't feel like work,' he told Music Week.

He denied that there had been any deliberate evolution in the sound of Harry's solo material. 'I don't know that there's ever been a conscious transition,' he said. 'The great thing about Harry is, he has so many ideas and he's the type of artist who knows exactly who he is. That makes our job a lot easier, all we try and do is be there and support him. Wherever it goes musically, we'll always try our best to push him as much as we can. No one is consciously saying we need to transition; we just give him the tools. We do our best to take it from there.'

As for Harry, he was basking in the freedom this brought him. 'While I was in the band,' he told Rolling Stone, 'I was constantly scared I might sing a wrong note. I felt so much weight in terms of not getting things wrong. I remember when I signed my record deal and I asked my manager, "What happens if I get arrested? Does it mean the contract is null and void?" Now, I feel like the fans have given me an environment to be myself and grow up and create this safe space to learn and make mistakes.'

The first Harry Styles solo song to be released was 'Sign Of The Times'. Speaking to National Public Radio, he explained the creation of the song. He said: 'I think I've always written bits of songs alone. And then I usually take stuff in and try and finish it with someone. And "Sign of the Times" was, like, one of those where I just kind of wrote it. We basically ended up in a place where the album had a bunch of, like, rock songs. We had a bunch of acoustic ballad songs. And I wrote "Sign of the Times", and that's the one that kind of started bridging us to different places in terms of experimenting a little more.'

He remembers when Simon Cowell phoned him with his verdict on the single. Although this was not quite as tense and defining as when Harry awaited Cowell's verdict on his first ever *X Factor* audition, he still hoped that his old mentor would approve. 'He said he really liked it and he was very proud of me,' remembered Harry. 'It was very friendly … not like past phone calls haven't been friendly, but I didn't get that nervy "the boss is calling" feel, which is nice.'

One person who was less than impressed with the track was Harry's former bandmate, Liam Payne. 'Sign of the Times' is not '[his] sort of music' and isn't something he'd listen to but he respects Harry's taste and thinks he 'did a great job of doing what he wanted to do. He'd say the same thing about me,' Payne said of Styles.

The pint-sized pop princess proudly proclaimed that Harry had written a 'beautiful' song for her second album.

Soon it would be time for Harry's solo debut album, but first there were some collaborations to be done. His first collaboration was with none other than the princess of pop herself, Ariana Grande. The pint-sized pop princess proudly proclaimed that Harry had written a 'beautiful' song for her second album. She said Harry penned the song 'Just A Little Bit Of Your Heart' after an entirely random encounter in the recording studio along with acclaimed producers Johan Carlsson and Savan Kotecha.

'I was at the studio one day and he was there, and literally, Johan and Savan were like, "Hey, do you want to write something for Ariana?" And (Harry) was like, "Sure, mate." And he just did,' she told MTV. 'It's a beautiful song. He's an amazing writer. It's really beautiful. He's amazingly talented.'

Then, he worked with Michael Bublé. The Canadian-Italian singer-songwriter has earned himself global fame for his crooning hits, like 'Me and Mrs Jones', 'It's a Beautiful Day' and 'Feeling Good'. His combination of reworked swing-era classics and original ballads has made him an instantly identifiable voice on the radio and at weddings.

Announcing his new song 'Someday', Bublé said: 'For the first time ever, I've recorded an original [song] that I didn't write. It's written by Meghan Trainor and Harry Styles.' Trainor remembered the experience well. She picked up her ukulele and sang in front of Harry. 'Performing a love song in front of Harry is terrifying, and on top of that I was a little nervous because he was one of the first celebrities I met,' she said.

'Harry was super-talented at writing, and his lyrics were incredible – probably my favourite lyrics in a song. I remember I wrote it at midnight the night before and sent it to my mom. I was so worried he was going to hate it. We finished the song in an hour or two and I love it. I was nervous 'cos I thought he'd be like a Justin Bieber, like "he's so famous" and love himself,' Meghan added, 'but he was just so normal … I immediately wasn't nervous any more.'

Showing how dexterous he could be, he also helped write a song for the American indie-pop band Bleachers. Harry co-wrote the track 'Alfie's Song (Not So Typical Love Song)', released as a single by the band, for the soundtrack of the film Love, Simon, which came out in 2018.

With all of this, he was working on the basis that to find the gold he would first have to rub through a lot of dirt. 'When I started I really didn't know what I was doing,' he admitted in i-D. 'So I tried to write as much as possible, with as many different people as possible and try and learn as much as I could. I guarantee I wrote a lot of really, really bad shit before I wrote anything good.'

It was a principle that worked. As far as many of his fans were concerned, Harry struck gold several times on his solo album. Another guiding rule for him was to really immerse himself in the project. With One Direction, recording would often be slotted in among all manner of other activities, such as interviews and appearances, but as a solo artist he could do one thing at a time. 'When I was in the band, I always knew what I was doing two years in advance,' Harry told *i-D*. 'Now, I'm making records on my own, it's pretty exciting because I know this is all I'm going to be doing until I finish the record. It's a new way of working.'

The album would be eponymous – named simply *Harry Styles*. However, it could have been different. Before naming the album after himself, he had considered a number of other titles for it. One name he mulled was *Pink*. Quoting Paul Simonon, the bassist of The Clash, he said: 'Pink is the only true rock and roll colour.' Harry also thought about naming it after the debut single, 'Sign of the Times'. This might have brought an era-defining claim to the album but Harry decided against it. 'I don't know. I mean, it has been used,' he said, with a nod to the well-known Prince album of the same name.

The experience of creating his solo debut was one that Harry had thoroughly enjoyed. He loved the extra time he was allowed to spend on his material as a solo artist. After all, songwriting was not something he was entirely new to: with One Direction, he had played a part in the composition of several of their songs, including 'Olivia', 'Stockholm Syndrome' and 'Happily'. He had had a hand in that part of the process and considered himself a songwriter, albeit a budding one.

However, the composition of those tracks had felt rushed. The merciless demands of the whole One Direction industry did not allow for a whole lot of reflection. 'We didn't get the six months to see what kind of shit you can work with,' he said. As a solo artist he was enjoying a different pace of composition and production – and he was basking in it. 'To have time to live with a song, see what you love as a fan, chip at it, hone it and go for that … it's heaven,' he said.

And as he made himself comfortable in that heaven, he was forever grasping for the authenticity of material that was true to his experiences. 'I didn't want to write "stories",' he told *Rolling Stone*. 'I wanted to write my stories, things that happened to me. The number-one thing was I wanted to be honest. I hadn't done that before.'

The aforementioned heaven was actually set over a trio of earthly locations. He recorded the tracks in three countries: England, the US and Jamaica. Most memorable for him was his time in Jamaica. For eight weeks in 2016, he was holed up in the remote Geejam studio near Port Antonio, a studio where pop royalty such as Rihanna and Drake have laid down tracks.

'I went there because I didn't want to be around distractions,' he told the *Independent*. 'The thing with being in London, or LA, or pretty much anywhere that you know people, is it's tough, because you go into the studio for ten hours, and then, at some point, everyone has to eat, and you go home.

'I just wanted to really dive into it and immerse myself. It became this fluid thing that we were just doing all of the time, rather than going in from nine to five. I also didn't want to be around people who might tell me what [the music] should sound like.'

He soon settled into something of a routine. At night, Harry and his guitarist, Rowland, stayed up and watched romantic comedies on Netflix. He particularly liked the films of Nicholas Sparks, who he now called 'Nicky Spee'. Eventually, as dawn broke, he would emerge bleary-eyed from the feel-good movie marathons, his mind full of the characters and plots. Hugh Grant's voice must have echoed in his head.

These were fun times on the island: his bandmates remember a heap of stories, including the time Harry got drunk and wet from the ocean, and began to toast everybody, wearing a dress he'd swapped with someone's girlfriend. 'I don't remember the toast,' he says, 'but I remember the feeling.' He made an impact on those who worked with him, Harry's easy-going charisma winning many hearts and minds.

He says the centrepiece of the album's lyrics is about a relationship he had recently come out of. 'She's a huge part of the album,' he said, of the unnamed partner who so influenced him. 'Sometimes you want to tip the hat, and sometimes you just want to give them the whole cap … and hope they know it's just for them.'

The media grapevine believes that the 'she' he is referring to is Kendall Jenner, the American model and media personality, but he has yet to confirm this. Was she the 'good girl' he sings of so passionately in 'Carolina', for instance? Speculation often goes into overdrive and we will examine plenty of it in Chapter Ten.

> The centrepiece of the album's lyrics is about a relationship he had recently come out of. 'She's a huge part of the album.'

When people talk and write about Harry's solo debut they often focus on how many retro flavours they can taste in the mix. However, although Harry loves listening to music from previous eras, it does not mean he wishes he lived in any of those past decades.

'A lot of my influences, and the stuff that I love, is older … I didn't want to put out my first album and be like, "He's tried to recreate the sixties, seventies, eighties, nineties." Loads of amazing music was written then, but I'm not saying I wish I lived back then. I wanted to do something that sounds like me.'

His producer, Jeff Bhasker, has offered his own take on what they had aimed for. 'It's different from what you'd expect. It made me realize the Harry [in 1D] was kind of the digitized Harry. Almost like a character. I don't think people know a lot of the sides of him that are on this album. You put it on and people are like, "This is Harry Styles?"'

After nearly seven years of the media obsessing about every aspect of his life, Harry enjoyed a new sensation when the critics responded to his first album. Here, a lot of them seemed to write about anything but the man himself. Instead, the reviews became a case of naming as many other artists and bands as they could, as writers strained themselves to identify influences in his songs.

This is not to say that there were not influences aplenty. Some of them were subtle and perhaps open to debate; others were somewhat clearer. However, for Harry, it might have felt disappointing to have the reviews mostly focused on this rather than his songwriting.

As well as the individual sum of its parts, *Harry Styles* is also fascinating for its whole and for the sequence in which those parts are put together. A lot of artists would never choose 'Meet Me in the Hallway' to open an album. With its gentle guitar and soft ambient beeps, it is a soft, melancholy affair. Harry sounds dozy as he delivers the lyrics about a couple who might work out their difficulties, but ultimately there is no redemption or grasping for reassuring positives. It doesn't grab the listener by the throat and is arguably the least remarkable track on the album. So putting it first breaks the usual rules of album track-listing but this isn't a 'usual' album.

Firstly, Harry is making a statement, establishing his creative credentials and casting off his boy-band background. Secondly, he is in a strong position: which One Direction fan buying the album would dream of switching off the album or skipping a track? 'Meet Me in the Hallway' is also thematically important, setting out the theme of the collection.

Echoes of those childhood spins of Pink Floyd's *The Dark Side of the Moon* album can be sensed here. However, the song is perfectly suited to his voice. He sounds positively dreamy in the chorus and as he asks to be given some morphine, it sounds like he's already imbibed a bit. *NME* said the song presented Harry as 'a windswept, lovesick LA troubadour, hurtling through Hollywood'.

If the opener recalled acts from the 1970s then track two, 'Sign of the Times', is a more nineties jam. Here are Robbie Williams, Oasis, Stereophonics and Starsailor. Although many critics thought they identified homages to David Bowie, much of the sound is more recent. With his talk of the final show and the end being near, this song is also apocalyptic, but never has the end of the world felt more stylish – Harry even sings that he hopes we're wearing our best clothes.

However, this is no four-minute warning: the song clocks in at nearly six minutes, which is bold at the best of times but even more so in a song picked to launch a solo career. The song's theme may

> 'I think it would have been weird for me to kind of write an album and not acknowledge that there's anything bad going on in the world.'

go over the heads of many listeners. As Harry later told *Rolling Stone* magazine: 'The song is written from a point of view as if a mother was giving birth to a child and there's a complication. The mother is told, "The child is fine, but you're not going to make it." The mother has five minutes to tell the child, "Go forth and conquer."'

He later explained to National Public Radio: 'I think it would have been weird for me to kind of write an album and not acknowledge that there's anything bad going on in the world. And I think we were just writing it from kind of a place of – all right, you have five minutes to kind of say it's going to be all right.'

After such a grand and sombre track comes a more playful and jaunty one, in the form of 'Carolina'. A rocky track with impish 'la la la la' backing vocals, it is Harry at his most fun and cheeky. After opening the album with a track about a troubled relationship and one about a dying mother, we needed a mood lightener for track three and we got it. As he sings that the song's heroine feels so good, so do we. It has something of the Beatles about it but rather than sounding like that band's cool John Lennon, here Harry sounds more like the cheeky Paul McCartney – and not for the last time on the album.

The mood sobers up immediately with track four: 'Two Ghosts'. Here, a couple have become the titular pair of ghosts, trying to remember how it felt to be in the passion of love, or how it felt to have a heartbeat, as he metaphorically puts it. Musically, it's middle-of-the-road, with tinges of country guitar. You could drive along an epic Midwest road on a baking day listening to this and everything would feel right.

Those with one ear on the music and the other on the celebrity grapevine will find their listening holes twitching in this song, which seems to nod to his rumoured fling with Taylor Swift and her own seeming nod to it in her own song, 'Style'.

He wrote this track way back in the One Direction days, but it never saw the light of day with the band. Instead, it had to wait for his solo effort. Harry is pleased it turned out that way. "'Two Ghosts" I wrote for the band, for *Made In The A.M.* But the story was just a bit too personal. As I started opening up to write my more personal stuff, I just became aware of a piece of me going, "I want to sing the whole thing." Now I look at a track list and these are all my little babies. So every time I'm playing a song, I can remember writing it, and exactly where we were and exactly what happened in my life when I wrote it. So the whole show is this massive emotional journey, you know? That's a big difference, rather than every twenty minutes you go, "Oh, I remember this one.'"

Harry hoped his solo album would appeal to a wider audience than his 1D army and on track five, the older end of his listenership will be identifying a different influence than that detected by his younger fans. From its opening acoustic lick, 'Sweet Creature' is immediately reminiscent of Beatles tracks 'Blackbird' and, to a lesser extent, 'Norwegian Wood'. Harry has returned to McCartney here, older listeners will feel. However, for the younger fans, this track will make them think of Ed Sheeran. It's easy to imagine the ginger crooner – responsible for similar tracks like 'Little Bird' – pinging out a song like this. *Amnplify*'s Cassandra Thomson wrote that the track's 'melody perfectly accompanies the soothingly strong vocals and genuinely sentimental and reflective lyrics of distant loves and relationships'.

Rolling Stone says 'Only Angel' sees him delve into 'hard rock raunch', and *Variety* describes it as 'raging rock'. While both descriptions may labour the point a little, compared to everything that comes before it this track certainly is a departure. As we have seen, Styles has often been compared to Mick Jagger visually.

With its wild 'woo hoo' backing vocals and its saucier lyrics, it is about a girl who masquerades as angelic but is, Harry tells us, a devil between the sheets. He sings of getting the song's heroine stuck between his teeth. The way this song leaps into life after a brief, gentle intro would make it an ideal album opener, in more conventional circumstances. It has, says *Variety*, a 'faint whiff of the Sunset Strip'.

The rockiness continues on the next track, 'Kiwi', which sounds like rock band Wolfmother. *DIY* magazine said that those with only a passing interest in Styles will find the track 'a jump into the deepest of deep ends'. This is one of the album's most criticized tracks. Many reviewers were simply unconvinced. *Variety* found it 'parodically sleazy and unconvincing' and the BBC said that though it is the 'loudest, rawest track on the album' it's also 'faintly ridiculous'.

EW was somewhat more positive, saying that 'Kiwi' and its predecessor are 'swaggering slabs of codpiece rock' that would beat up gentler tracks, such as 'Two Ghosts', in the bathroom. The one-two punch of these two songs sets the album up for a more expansive second half.

Gigwise compared it to heavy-metal legends AC/DC and worried aloud: 'Is this what sixty-odd years of rock music history is to be reduced to in the minds of 2017's impressionable pop kids?' Perhaps, though, the biggest influence is a more recent one: that of the noughties indie two-piece, the White Stripes.

'Ever Since New York' sees the album return to its gentler opening. 'The song is pure rock troubadour,' chirps *Variety*. *Hey Nineteen* says it is 'another soft-rock affair, a mid-tempo track built on a mesh of interweaving guitars' that shows 'Styles is aiming for something mature here, going for a slow burner rather than a quick pop fix'.

However, many critics felt it would have benefitted from a bit more life and energy, and a more distinct chorus. While some will have welcomed the dip into mellower terrain, others found it boring. The BBC, for instance, described it as 'pretty stodgy stuff, elevated only by Harry's supple backing vocals'. It also created a kerfuffle when it was compared to the 1970s hit 'Baby Blue' by Badfinger. Some began to say the song was not so much influenced by the track, but actively copied it.

Fan theories abounded here – with people wondering if the song was about his reported fling with Taylor Swift. One of the pair's more iconic moments was a walk through Central Park in New York City, a moment that was photographed widely and was tabloid fodder all over the world. A fact of life of twenty-first-century pop, and its increasing tie-in with celebrity culture, is the analysis – and sometimes overanalysis – of songs' lyrics.

Then we arrive at the album's more divisive offerings: 'Woman'. *Pitchfork* called it 'laughable', the BBC said it features 'what appears to be an asthmatic duck' and the *NME* said it had 'wonky honks', but the *Observer* said 'it's a bitter grizzle about imagining your ex with someone else, and it is great'.

It has been compared to everything from Prince to Joe Walsh and Elton John. Rich with funk rock and hints of modern R&B, it is a memorable track. A song about jealousy and the pain of possessiveness, it is perhaps most reminiscent of John Lennon. One thing is for sure: it captured the imagination.

'From the Dining Table' takes us back in many ways to where the album started: a gentle track about a relationship gone wrong. Although we began in the hallway and ended at the dining table, the mood and predicament is much the same.

Here, though, the lyrics are more open and confessional: he sings of playing with himself in a hotel bed and getting drunk before noon, and says his phone is missing the calls from his lost lover. He is tortured here and though there is a moment of optimism, the song – and album – ends with him heartbroken and alone. It's quite a distance from 1D's pop hit 'Best Song Ever'. *NME* said it was 'as intimate as anything on Bon Iver's first album'.

In the vulnerability and lack of pretence of the lyrics, he was aiming for something important. 'I don't think people want to hear me talk about going to bars, and how great everything is. The champagne popping … who wants to hear about it?' he said to *Rolling Stone*.

> 'I don't think people want to hear me talk about going to bars, and how great everything is. The champagne popping … who wants to hear about it?'

'I don't want to hear my favourite artists talk about all the amazing shit they get to do. I want to hear, "How did you feel when you were alone in that hotel room, because you chose to be alone?"'

For Harry, 'From the Dining Table' was his favourite track on the album. 'It's just personal, and I don't feel like I've written a song like this before,' he said. 'I'd say it's the most honest I've been. I've never written and recorded a song like that. The song at a time when any barrier of editing myself is stripped away. I never do anything while

I listen to it, it's a song that makes me stop and listen rather than doing something and having it on in the background.'

As for critics' assessments of the album in general, these were mixed. The *Daily Telegraph* was critical, comparing it to Paul McCartney's first solo album, but only in the sense that the Macca collection was 'rambling' and 'almost provocatively amateurish'. There is, it adds, 'do-as-you-please music making' and 'silly rhymes'.

Alexis Petridis of the *Guardian* felt that while 'Styles is remarkably good as a confessional singer-songwriter … not all the album's musical homages work'. Another critic was Mesfin Fekadu of *Associated Press*, who noted that the performance aspect of the album is where Styles 'truly shines', but 'not so much' in the creative process.

Leonie Cooper of *NME* looked at how the album would be received by those outside Harry's existing and traditional fan base. The hard-core fans, wrote Cooper, would be 'over the moon with this collection of radio-friendly rockers and heartstring tugging balladry' and 'everyone else' will 'be pleasantly surprised – if not a little taken aback at just how many tricks he's pinched from other artists'.

Rolling Stone concluded that Harry 'claims his turf as a true rock & roll prince' on his 'superb solo debut', while his regular champion Mikael Wood of the *Los Angeles Times* wrote that he 'never overplays his hand on this winningly relaxed collection' which was 'full of echoes of the Beatles, Pink Floyd and the Rolling Stones'.

Billboard said Harry 'has opted to forego radio play and make a big, brash guitar album', adding, 'his commitment to conjuring the spirit of '70s rock never comes across as overreaching'.

The pre-release promotion for the album had been exciting. The album name, artwork and track list were revealed on 13 April 2017. The front cover showed Harry bathing with his back exposed for all his admirers to see. The track 'Sweet Creature' was released as a promotional single on 2 May.

Then came the television appearances. Harry sang 'Sign of the Times' and 'Ever Since New York' on *Saturday Night Live* on 15 April.

Six days later, he appeared on the BBC's *Graham Norton Show* for his first televised solo performance in the UK. Five days later he guested on the French talk show *Quotidien*, singing 'Sign of the Times'. With the album release just three days away, he was back in the US, where he performed 'Carolina', 'Sign of the Times', 'Ever Since New York' and a cover of One Direction's 'Stockholm Syndrome' on *The Today Show*. He appeared as a guest on *The Late Late Show* with his old mate James Corden every night between 15 and 18 May.

The album went straight to the top of the UK Albums Chart thanks to first-week sales of 57,000 units.

Upon its release, the album went straight to the top of the UK Albums Chart thanks to first-week sales of 57,000 units. Harry had done it: he had become the second One Direction member to achieve a number-one solo album, following Zayn Malik's *Mind of Mine* in April 2016.

Across the pond, it also debuted at the top, going straight to number one in the US *Billboard* 200 with 230,000 album-equivalent units. This made it the highest first-week sales for a British male artist's debut full-length album since Nielsen SoundScan began in 1991, beating Sam Smith's *In the Lonely Hour* (2014), which moved 166,000 copies in its first week.

Harry could be proud of the work and of reactions to it.

CHAPTER SIX

ON
THE ROAD

With the album released, Harry hit the road to promote it. It was here that he would truly feel the reality of the solitude of the solo life. In the studio with One Direction, he was used to laying down his parts of the vocals alone. Tracks are put together in pieces that are then welded together by the deft hands of the production team, so recording a solo album wasn't that different from the process of recording a 1D album.

However, onstage, the solo artist cannot help but notice how alone they are and how much depends on them. In arenas the stages are big and the audiences are vast. However many band members, backing singers or even dancers the solo artist deploys for live shows, they know that everything really depends on them and whether they deliver on the night.

During the preparations and rehearsals for his first tour, Harry's mind was transported back to 2011, when he and his fellow 1D members got ready for their first tour. Although he was by now a seasoned professional in many ways, he was also fresh and excited about the prospect of a solo tour. Much of what lay ahead was predictable and familiar to Harry, but some of it would be uncharted territory.

He would take to the stage and the roof would nearly fall in with the hysteria of the fans. 'I have one job tonight and that's to entertain you.'

Although there were some tweaks and evolution throughout the tour, a certain amount of the show would remain the same every night. At the shows, before he took to the stage, the PA would play an interesting collection of songs. There would be a bit of Shania Twain and then Stephen Stills' 'Love the One You're With', before Queen's 'Bohemian Rhapsody' and One Direction's 'Olivia'. In a procession perhaps never considered by anyone at all before these shows, 1D would merge into Pink Floyd, with their thhirteen-minute track 'Shine On You Crazy Diamond'.

Then, Van Morrison's 'Madame George' would blare out of the speakers. The ten-minute track is about a Belfast drag queen. It had been quite a build-up of tracks that reflected Harry's diverse taste in music before he appeared. Then, he would take to the stage and the roof would nearly fall in with the hysteria of the fans. 'I have one job tonight and that's to entertain you,' he would say. It was a bold mission statement, similar to the one Robbie Williams would sometimes utter at the beginning of his solo gigs.

With his band of Mitchell Rowland on guitar and vocals, Clare Uchima on keyboards and vocals, plus Sarah Jones on drums and vocals and Adam Prendergast on bass and vocals, he then set about doing just that – entertaining and thrilling the audience.

There was great excitement over how his set list would run. Harry's shows began with an opening trio of 'Only Angel', 'Woman' and 'Ever Since New York'. Then came 'Two Ghosts' and 'Carolina', followed by a nod back to the days of One Direction in the form of 'Stockholm Syndrome'. The show then proceeded with 'Just a Little Bit of Your Heart', 'Medicine' and 'Meet Me in the Hallway'.

Next up came the cute 'Sweet Creature', 'If I Could Fly' and 'Anna'. The main body of the show came to a glorious climax with 'What Makes You Beautiful' and 'Sign of the Times'. His encores included 'From the Dining Table' and a cover of Fleetwood Mac's 'The Chain', before the show concluded with the strutting fun of 'Kiwi'.

There had been some debate over whether or not he should play One Direction songs on the tour. Tom Hull, also known as Kid Harpoon and who wrote some of the songs on the album, explained that at first Harry was 'cautiously up for it'. Hull added: 'I feel like those One Direction songs are brilliantly written songs, and obviously it was a moment where we had a conversation. Beyoncé does Destiny's Child songs, so we were like, "Let's do some of the songs that people will all know and everyone will love."' However, for 'What Makes You Beautiful', Harry wanted to make sure that he pumped out a different take on the song as a solo artist. It was decided, said Hull, to give it a 'Ray Charles-y vibe' and a 'Motown-y beat'.

The most memorable part of the shows was not the songs themselves, but the lovely and loving atmosphere Harry would conjure.

For many, the most memorable part of the shows was not the songs themselves, but the lovely and loving atmosphere Harry would conjure. These were truly inclusive events. 'Please feel free to be whoever it is you choose to be in this room tonight,' he told the crowd at his sold-out show at New York's Madison Square Garden, and many of the other dates on the road. To drive home the point, he wrapped himself in the rainbow flag and the bi-pride flag. As he introduced his debut single in NYC, he said: 'This song is for anyone out there who needs it. This is "Sign of the Times". Happy Pride!'

As several reviewers of that Manhattan show noted, Harry didn't even make it to the chorus of the first song before he spun round to blow kisses at the fans seated behind the stage. He wanted them to know that even though there were behind him for most of the show they were as important to him as anyone else in the audience that night. 'That's not just shrewd stagecraft; that's a philosophical statement,' said *Rolling Stone*. 'His generous spirit was contagious all night.'

Harry was excited for the shows in his home nation. When he hit London, he played the vast O2 arena. He appeared to deafening screams, wearing a pink, embellished jacket and matador-style spangly trousers. One observer felt he looked like Freddie Mercury. Perhaps no other act will ever quite match the Queen lead singer's charisma, but Harry's presence was strong.

At all his shows he blew kisses to individual audience members, paused to hold eye contact with a lucky few and offered birthday shout-outs. Having announced individual fans' birthdays early in the show, as the gigs reached their glorious climaxes he would repeat the names of the birthday celebrators. This feat of memory really put the icing on the cake.

His individual touch was a true winner for those in the seats. He also tailored his banter to where he was playing. When he played Dublin, he told a story about getting headbutted in Tallaght. He also remarked off the cuff that 'Kildare is beautiful this time of year' when one fan shouted out her county pride. Veering between gigantic icon and everyman, he made the shows true rock events and cosy chats all at once.

ABOVE A new look for a new solo career, London, 2016.

LEFT On location filming *Dunkirk*, UK, 2016.

BELOW A scene from the film featuring Harry with Aneurin Barnard and Fionn Whitehead.

ABOVE Harry arrives in style at the world premiere of *Dunkirk* at the Odeon, Leicester Square, London, 2017.

BELOW When Harry met Prince Harry at the film premiere of *Dunkirk*.

ABOVE Performing on the NBC's *The Today Show* at Rockefeller Center, New York, 2017.

BELOW A star in his own right, Harry appears on *The Tonight Show with Jimmy Fallon*, New York.

ABOVE With only two hours' notice, Harry fills in for James Corden on his show after James's wife goes into labour!

BELOW Spotify celebrates the launch of Harry's new album *Fine Line* with a private listening session for fans, 2019.

LEFT Modelling for iconic brand Gucci in Rome.

BELOW Harry looking fabulous as he attends the Met Gala, New York, 2019.

LEFT Bringing pearls back into fashion – Harry at the 40th BRIT Awards, The O2 Arena, London, 2020.

BELOW The following year, Harry won the Best British Single Award for 'Watermelon Sugar'.

ABOVE In May 2022 Harry performed at Radio 1's Big Weekend in Coventry.

BELOW Gemma Chan, Harry Styles, Sydney Chandler, Olivia Wilde and Chris Pine attend the *Don't Worry Darling* red carpet event at the 79th Venice International Film Festival in September 2022.

Here, too, he played the inclusive card, as noted by the *Independent*'s Sabrina Barr. 'Styles made sure to spread the love throughout the night, chatting with an array of his most avid followers and proudly gracing the stage with rainbow-coloured flags,' she wrote. The *Irish Times* was impressed by the poise of all this. 'Styles may be in the early stages of his solo career but with performances like this, it's clear that he's in it for the long run,' they wrote.

The responses to his live shows from heavyweight publications were an absolute triumph for Harry. When an artist fresh out of One Direction is being lauded by the likes of the *Los Angeles Times*, you know they have nailed the transition from boy band to serious solo credibility.

'Nothing is more boring than the perpetual conversation about whether rock is dead,' wrote August Brown in that very journal. 'But if you're gonna enter that fracas, take note – Harry Styles is probably one of the genre's finest practitioners at the moment, and one of its most ideologically modern as well.'

Esquire, the grown-up men's mag, was also blown away. 'A Harry Styles concert gave me faith in the youths,' wrote Matt Miller. Only a soul as generous as Harry could perform a concert that ended with a positive review not only for him but for an entire generation. 'It's easy – so easy – to look at the Tide Pod generation and be worried. It's easy to think that kids are just going to play whatever *Fortnite* is while the world burns around them,' wrote Miller. 'But then there's Harry Styles, who's here to remind us that youths are here, they're aware, and they actually care.'

For Harry, the entire experience changed his life. It was here that he felt true and deep acceptance. When the tour dates originally went on sale, they sold out in a matter of seconds in twenty-nine different countries. The pre-sale for the concert at Mall of Asia Arena in Manila broke Coldplay's record of six minutes by selling out in less than one minute – just fifty-two seconds. 'I am overwhelmed, thank you,' he wrote on Twitter. 'If I don't get to see you on this tour, I'll come back around next year if you'll have me. Love, H.'

Across two legs, he played thirty-six dates in North America, thirty-one in Europe and nine in Asia. In Australia he played seven shows and there were six in Latin America, bringing the tour in total to eighty-nine nights. 'The first few gigs we ever did as One Direction, in some nightclubs, girls were fainting and getting pulled out of the audience. We thought it was one of the strangest things we ever saw. I didn't think any of us would get used to the screaming, and that reaction. It's just mad!

'It made me realize people want to see me experiment and have fun. Nobody wants to see you fake it.'

'The tour, that affected me deeply. It really changed me emotionally. Having people come to sing the songs. For me the tour was the biggest thing in terms of being more accepting of myself, I think. I kept thinking, "Oh wow, they really want me to be myself. And be out and do it." That's the thing I'm most thankful for, of touring. The fans in the room [make] this environment where people come to feel like they can be themselves. There's nothing that makes me feel more myself than to be in this whole room of people. It made me realize people want to see me experiment and have fun. Nobody wants to see you fake it.'

The reviews of the concerts included passages that you could never in a million years have expected to read in a live review of One Direction, however long the band had stayed together. 'Night after night, Harry Styles is taking on the central pop-culture question of our moment: What does it mean to share joy, on a mass level, at a time when every day brings a constant barrage of rage? What does it mean to gather a pop tribe and then treat this tribe with respect and affection?' remarked *Rolling Stone*'s Rob Sheffield. *Billboard* said, 'subtlety is Harry Styles's ace', adding: 'He is very, very good at being subtle.'

It had been a major money-making experience. Record amounts of merchandise were sold in over fifty venues in North and South America, Australia and Europe, according to Live Nation. But most important was the value of the esteem Harry took from the tour. He had set off feeling nervous and vulnerable, but also excited and determined. The responses of the audiences at the shows told him all he needed to know about how respected he is as a solo artist.

Meanwhile, the portfolio career he was building for himself had gained another entry. Harry had moved into the world of acting – and he had entered the building through its most star-studded of doors.

CHAPTER SEVEN

PLAYING UP

Harry did not take a gentle route into acting. Not for him the bit part in an indie movie to ease him into the world of cinema. Instead, he debuted in a major blockbuster, Christopher Nolan's wartime epic *Dunkirk*, a film that was truly gruelling to shoot. 'There was one day when we were filming, where we were swimming nearby one of the larger boats – I think that was the day there was the most number of things going crazy,' he remembered.

'There was a boat blowing up as you were swimming, there were bullet noises everywhere, there was fire, people screaming and cameramen screaming … There was a lot going on. There was a bit where you're like, are we filming? What just happened?'

★ ★ ★

There is a fine tradition of pop stars moving into acting. Going back to the 1960s, Elvis Presley acted in countless films including *Harum Scarum* and *Stay Away, Joe*. In later decades, Michael Jackson appeared in such films as *The Wiz* and *Men in Black II*. Madonna was in in *Evita* and *A League of Their Own*. More recently, Jennifer Lopez has appeared in such films as *Maid in Manhattan*, *The Boy Next Door* and the critically acclaimed *Hustlers*. Beyoncé appeared in *Dreamgirls*, Justin Timberlake appeared in *Alpha Dog* and *The Social Network* and Lady Gaga was nominated for an Oscar for her standout performance in *A Star is Born*.

It's fair to say that these appearances have provoked very mixed reactions. Many have praised the pop singers for their acting chops but there have also been plenty of critics ready to be snarky and put the boot in. Often, the singers have emerged from the experience feeling they were judged unfairly – by a higher standard than they would have been had they not found fame first as a pop singer.

> 'They're almost opposite for me. Music, you try and put so much of yourself into it; acting, you're trying to totally disappear in whoever you're being.'

It was down this well-trodden path that Harry walked when he moved into the acting industry. It would be a satisfying and well-received journey. After mega-fame arrived at his doorstep at the age of sixteen, making him feel perpetually exposed to the entire universe, it was perhaps not surprising that Harry was attracted to the element of retreat offered by acting – it must have been refreshing to be someone other than 'Harry Styles from One Direction', for a little while at least.

'Why do I want to act? It's so different to music for me,' he said. 'They're almost opposite for me. Music, you try and put so much of yourself into it; acting, you're trying to totally disappear in whoever you're being.'

Having stated his desire to disappear into someone, the first person he got to disappear into was Alex in the war movie *Dunkirk*. The film sees Harry wade through mud as a soldier during the evacuation of 338,000 Allied troops after France was overrun by the Nazis in 1940. Those troops were surrounded by the enemy on a beach in France, with the English Channel their only escape route home.

Harry's character Alex is saved by another soldier from a ship that is sinking after an attack by dive-bombers. Alex then gets sunk again and saved again, and he and the other man end up on the beach. They hide from the Germans inside a beached trawler outside the Allied perimeter.

'He's in the film almost right up to the very end, when he gets an emotional scene on a train that proves him to be quite a fine little actor.'

The first question that a lot of Harry's fans had was whether he dies, but although he comes close to death at various points he prevails. As *Variety* put it: 'And not only does he not die, he's in the film almost right up to the very end, when he gets an emotional scene on a train that proves him to be quite a fine little actor.' He even gets to read about the Battle of Dunkirk in the newspaper.

The film would also star such names as Tom Hardy, Cillian Murphy, Fionn Whitehead and Kenneth Branagh. Its director, Christopher Nolan, who had previously conjured such gems as *Interstellar*, *Inception* and *The Dark Knight*, had first thought of the idea for the film in the mid-1990s, when Harry was still at primary school.

Harry was a fan of Nolan's cult film *Memento*, so he was excited to work with him. As for the director, he knew that there was a degree of gambling involved in the premise of the film, especially for the commercially paramount US audiences, who would have little knowledge of the event. Nevertheless, the trailer declared that the film would tell the story of 'the event that shaped our world'. There was also a gamble involved in the casting of Harry as he was completely unknown as an actor; but it was a bet that paid off.

Filming took place in 2016. Nolan opted for an immersive style, taking the audience into the heart of the action. This only intensified the challenge for Harry and his fellow cast members. Much of the filming took place in Dunkirk – at the location of the real evacuation. 'When they told me we were doing a movie on a beach, I had very different ideas!' he said. 'I definitely enjoyed playing someone else. I loved being so far out of my comfort zone. I loved being on set and being the guy who had no idea what he was doing. I really enjoyed that.'

In a scene where he ate jam and bread he ended up stuffed. He was told there was a 'spit bucket' in which he could dispose of the food, so he wouldn't have to fill up at every take, but he was told this 'way too late' and he was already feeling 'a little jammy'.

He told the *Big Issue*: 'All of history is why we are where we are … And I think when you can tell a part of that, a part that is often overlooked, it's important to do that rather than focusing on the end chapter, which obviously seems much more significant. But a lot of things happened to get to those places, so I think focusing on a very important set of events in history and telling that part of the story is really important.'

A major change in his appearance was necessary for the film – he had to have his long locks of hair cut. He said he didn't 'really think' about having to make the change because he was 'very excited to be getting to set and being involved and working on [the film]'. He added that 'it kind of went without saying', and even quipped that having shorter hair for the first time in years also had its perks. 'It was a little breezy behind the ears, which was nice,' he laughed.

'It's hard to know what to expect walking into an environment like that – and it was amazing,' he told the *Big Issue*. 'The first surprising thing was the scale of the production. You walk on set the first day and get taken aback by everything.'

'Harry was absolutely right for the role. As an actor he is unknown, but his readings made him an obvious choice.'

Of the film's esteemed director, Harry said: '[Nolan] never makes you feel like you have to try too hard. He wants it to be like you're saying stuff for the first time and doing stuff for the first time – because you are. In terms of first-day memories, we finished one shot and he said, "Congrats on your first close-up." It was good.

'Chris kind of creates this world view where you don't have to act that much. He tries to make it so he is capturing natural reactions to stuff.'

Co-star Jack Lowden, who plays RAF pilot Collins, said: 'It's admirable that the guy's having a pop, I guess he's today's equivalent of a Beatle. I think he got on well.'

He also insists Nolan would not cast anybody who might not be good enough: 'That man knows what he's doing.'

The casting director, John Papsidera, told the *Mirror*: 'Harry was absolutely right for the role. As an actor he is unknown, but his readings made him an obvious choice. We thought he was fresh and interesting and he won the role.'

He denied that Harry's pop fame gave him a leg-up into the part. 'It wasn't because he's a well-known pop star – if anything that was more of a detriment, because it could bring the wrong message and we don't want people pulled out of the film because of who they are.

'So Harry really had to overcome hurdles to get past that. He fought hard for it and his work was impressive and that's what attracted us to him. I don't think he studied acting professionally and yet he won the role against some very well-known actors.

'This is a young man who passionately wanted this film and we looked at a lot of actors, certainly in the hundreds, some of them very well known and many who had been to prestigious acting schools. I have never gone to his concerts, listened to his music or anything like that. None of us had. Chris's kids knew who he was and we knew of him but we aren't followers of his career. It is absolutely his own talent, ambition and hard work that has got him a part in a Christopher Nolan movie.'

So to what extent did Harry empathize with the soldier experience he was portraying? 'I think it's impossible to ever feel what everyone involved was going through,' he said. 'It's tough to say we know what it was like because we don't but I think in terms of the environment you are in, it helped us get a sense of how uncomfortable it might have been.'

Nonetheless, Harry had put in an authentic performance. Nolan told the BBC: 'He's very, very real in what he does in the film, which is what I wanted. It's very truthful. But it's not glamorous. He's not an exotic villain, there's nothing obvious that he gets to do – you're playing human frailty. I think it would be hard to come away from a film like this, about what it's about, and not take a little piece of that with you.'

'He's very, very real in what he does in the film, which is what I wanted. It's very truthful. But it's not glamorous. He's not an exotic villain, there's nothing obvious that he gets to do – you're playing human frailty.'

Harry was just as admiring when he spoke of Nolan. 'I've always been such a massive fan of Christopher Nolan too … when he was sitting at the back of the room while I was auditioning, I felt very lucky to even be in that room. *Dunkirk* was strange because it was my first film, so I didn't have anything to compare it to.'

During a joint interview with his castmate Fionn Whitehead, Harry said: 'I think the thing is, it was really exciting to explore the relationship between the two characters. And how the tension would build and how each character would react differently to what they thought their role would be in the war and what their role was really like. I think exploring that was the most fun part for us.

'I think any time you get to be around people who you're a fan of and who are obviously passionate about what they do, it feels like a privilege. You just try and soak up as much as you can and use it as a learning experience.'

Fionn agreed that they bonded 'quite quickly'.

Harry would get thumbs-ups all round for his performance. Niall Horan, Harry's old bandmate, was massively impressed by his move. 'I'll tell you what, if Christopher Nolan takes you on, you must be a good actor,' he said. 'I think Harry is going to do well.'

'To his credit, his portrayal of a British soldier cowering in a moored boat on the French beaches as the Nazis advanced wasn't skewered in the press like the movie debuts of, say, Madonna or Justin Timberlake,' said *The Face*.

'He was brilliant in *Dunkirk*, which took a lot of people by surprise,' said Elton John. 'I love how he takes chances and risks.' The *Chicago Sun-Times* praised Harry for his 'fine work' and *Entertainment Weekly* said he was 'solid, seamlessly blending into the ensemble'.

'It's not enough to say that *Dunkirk* is Christopher Nolan's best film,' added the *San Francisco Chronicle*. 'It's one of the best war films ever made.'

Not everyone was sold on the film, though. The *Guardian* said it was 'bloodless, boring and empty', while *The Times* described it as '106 clamorous minutes of big-screen bombast that's so concerned with its own spectacle and scale that it neglects to deliver the most crucial element – drama'. The *Daily Telegraph*'s Robbie Collin praised

Harry for his 'bright, convicted, and unexpectedly not-at-all jarring performance'.

It received eight nominations at the 23rd Critics' Choice Awards. The gongs were for Best Picture, Best Director, Best Acting Ensemble, Best Cinematography, Best Editing, Best Visual Effects, Best Score and Best Production Design.

Attention then turned to which acting part Harry would take next. He reportedly came close to being cast as none other than Elvis Presley in Baz Luhrmann's biopic of the King of Rock 'n' Roll.

As *The Face* magazine's Trey Taylor put it: 'Makes complete sense that he would be up for the role of Elvis Presley in Baz Luhrmann's upcoming biopic. He was primed, nay, born to shake his hips, all but one button on his shirt clinging for dear life around his torso.'

> He reportedly came close to being cast as none other than Elvis Presley in Baz Luhrmann's biopic of the King of Rock 'n' Roll.

The possibility came close enough for Harry to start researching Presley's life, in preparation for a possible casting. '[Elvis] was such an icon for me growing up,' he told an interviewer. 'There was something almost sacred about him, almost like I didn't want to touch him. Then I ended up getting into [his life] a bit and I wasn't disappointed,' he added of his initial research and preparations to play the King.

However, the part was eventually handed to another actor, Austin Butler. Harry was philosophical about missing out. 'I feel like if I'm not the right person for the thing, then it's best for both of us that I don't do it, you know?' he said.

The uncertainty of Hollywood was driven home for Harry when he was considered for the role of Prince Eric in Disney's live-action remake of *The Little Mermaid*, only to see that also fall through. 'It was discussed,' he said. 'Everyone's told me that whatever I work on next will be a walk in the park compared to *Dunkirk*, but I enjoyed it. I want to put music out and focus on that for a while,' he went on. 'But everyone involved in it was amazing, so I think it's going to be great. I'll enjoy watching it, I'm sure.'

Harry was happy for the time being to look back at his experience on *Dunkirk*. 'Even with the drowning scenes, I quite enjoyed it, to be honest,' he told *USA Today*. 'I'd do it again.'

At the time of writing Harry hasn't been cast in any new films, but it seems certain that we will see him acting on the big screen again soon as in November 2020 it was rumoured that he was being lined up to star alongside Lily James in an adaptation of the LGBTQ+ novel, *My Policeman*. In the Amazon Studios movie he was expected to play a policeman called Tom, the love interest of James' character Marion. The plot thickens when Tom also falls in love with Patrick, a museum curator. Just the sort of storyline that would appeal to Harry's varied fanbase.

CHAPTER EIGHT

FASHION DARLING

Pink suits. Satin and Hawaiian shirts. Leather boots, silk scarves, chains and chunky rings, cowboy boots and tight jeans. These are just some of the signature garments and accessories that have become synonymous with Harry over the years. For a boy who spent the first year of his fame decked out in high-street-chain outfits, it has been quite an evolution.

But all along, Harry has gone in his own direction. Even as the band were still together, he was developing his own style and striking a much stronger pose onstage. He was towering over the others sartorially, unabashed in his ambition to become the superstar of the pack. He was in no mood to worry about outshining anyone with his style – his very name showed that he was always going to be a bit special when it came to sartorial grandeur. During his solo years, his interest in and passion for fashion have taken off – big time.

'Harry has always been keen to experiment with fashion and is never scared to try something new,' said his long-time stylist Harry Lambert. 'Over the years we have worked out what he likes and doesn't like. It has been a natural progression of experimentation that has led up to the look and where we are today.'

That progression and experimentation began long before he became an official 'fashionista'. As far back as 2013, Harry was the winner of the British Style Award – a gong that recognizes 'an individual who most embodies the spirit of London and is an international ambassador for London as a leading creative fashion capital'. As he accepted his award, he was grateful but brief. 'This is very, very kind,' he said.

By the following year, his sense of personal style was making itself more felt. Harry would be spotted clad in Hedi Slimane's Saint Laurent label. He also donned printed shirts, Wyatt boots and silk scarves. For a guy in a band who began wearing hoodies and onesies – the definition of a day's shopping in Topman – this was quite the evolution. From being dressed by the high street, he was now being styled by the catwalk.

Then, in 2015, the lid was blown off the whole fashion project. He turned up to the American Music Awards in a full Gucci runway look. A black and white floral jacquard suit, with flared trousers and a black shirt.

look. A black and white floral jacquard suit, with flared trousers and a black shirt. Combined with Harry's flowing locks, this made for a standout look on the red carpet. The other members of the band turned up in normal suits. Normal suits that cost a lot of money, but still garments that were left in the shade by Harry's floral number.

The photographs of them arriving at the show tell so many

stories about Harry and his relationship with the rest of the band. The other three look pensive and ordinary next to Harry, who looks casual, confident and charismatic. It is as if he has already checked out of One Direction and is, in his head, already in the new, promised land he was creating.

The media reaction was huge. The *Loop* said Harry 'wore an Ikea duvet' to the awards, while the *Sun* said he was 'slammed' for his outfit. MTV said it was a 'bold statement'. *Page Six* asked: 'WTF is Harry Styles wearing?' It had certainly captured the imagination. As the BBC said: 'He definitely stood out.'

However, while some of the coverage was snarky, Harry also got praise from more fashion-forward publications. *Teen Vogue* said: 'It's hard enough for women to take a fashion risk on the red carpet, when a misstep can mean being torn apart in magazines for years. It's a completely different ballgame for a man, whose red carpet options are typically incredibly limited and, let's face it, boring.'

It was a good point. Tyler McCall continued: 'When a man steps out in a bold, unexpected suit like Harry's, he can face more than just being mocked on the internet – it can also raise a lot of (unnecessary!) speculation about his sexuality. That's because our society dictates that masculinity and sexuality is defined by silly things, like what you wear, instead of how you identify yourself. So when Harry steps out in a floral suit or a pair of glittery boots, he's wearing what makes him happy without worrying about what people will think. That's something we should all applaud.'

It truly was an eye-popping suit with its flared trousers and classy jacket. Harry completed the look with some iconic cowboy boots. For the man himself, it marked something of a mental liberation. 'I used to wear all black all of the time … but I was realizing [dressing up] was a part of the show, if you will,' he told *Billboard*. 'Especially when performing. So, I think [for] the people I have always admired and looked up to in music, clothes have always been a big part of the thing. Like Bowie, Elvis Presley. It's always been part of the thing.'

Lambert, his stylist, confirms that this was indeed the 'turning point' for Harry and the beginning of what would become a long relationship with Gucci. 'It was very exciting to see everyone's responses, but also how great he looked in it. At the time it was a very bold move to make.' It was. As *Bustle* put it, the 'entire internet freaked out' when Harry's clothes were revealed. It added: 'It may resemble your grandmother's couch just a little, but the matching separates are working for me … Styles pretty much takes the cake.'

The reaction was widespread, itself a triumph for Harry. The *Daily Telegraph* described it as 'eye-catching', *Hollywood Reporter* said it was 'bold' and *Complex* said it was 'granny panty-dropping'. Some tweeters compared it to 'bathroom wallpaper and floral armchairs'. *Cosmopolitan* said it was 'one good-looking bedspread'. A lot of admiration, some disbelief and not a little mockery – one thing was for sure, everyone was talking about it.

✷ ✷ ✷

When Harry wears clothes like this it is important in many ways. As *Her Campus* put it: 'Harry Styles in a floral print Gucci suit makes my knees weak. Some people might giggle at the idea, not used to the sweet softness of a boy in pastels. This is what sets Styles apart from his male pop star peers: He's not afraid to embrace what's feminine.'

It argued that he was 'defying toxic masculinity', adding: 'the statement is this: Boys can enjoy what is soft and feminine and be joyful about it.' Zooming in on Harry's male fans, it said: 'The process of self-reflection caused by Styles's more feminine presentation can be a healthy, explorative time for boys and men to decide if there are things they've been missing out on because they were afraid of being too "girly".'

Fashion designer Harris Reed thought Harry was just the person for their inclusive, gender-fluid designs. 'Being someone who identifies as gender fluid, I've always seen it as important to put as much of myself into the work as inspiration,' said Reed.

'I don't think a man or a woman, someone who identifies as non-binary, or anywhere on the spectrum, has to dress in a certain way. I like the playfulness, the flounciness, of flares and billowy sleeves. I want to redefine the way we look at, say, a man who goes to work in a suit and a woman who goes to work in a skirt. Why can't you wear a fabulous sheer kaftan, or a pirate blouse? People should be able to express who they are.'

Toxic masculinity has been defined by the *New York Times* as a set of behaviours and beliefs that include: suppressing emotions or masking distress, maintaining an appearance of hardness, and violence as an indicator of power.

> 'He is telling men that they can wear what they want to wear, delve into themselves and pin their hearts firmly on their sleeves.'

'In other words,' wrote Maya Salam, 'toxic masculinity is what can come of teaching boys that they can't express emotion openly; that they have to be "tough all the time"; that anything other than that makes them "feminine" or weak.'

Urban Dictionary says: 'A social science term that describes [a] narrow repressive type of ideas about the male gender role, that defines masculinity as exaggerated masculine traits like being violent, unemotional, sexually aggressive, and so forth. Also suggests that men who act too emotional or maybe aren't violent enough or don't do all of the things that "real men" do, can get their "man card" taken away.'

So is this a trend that Harry is helping to disperse? On this, there is hot debate. Many believe he is. As *Grazia* put it: 'He is telling men that they can wear what they want to wear, delve into themselves and pin their hearts firmly on their sleeves. It may seem small, but it is truly life-changing. And that is why I will keep wearing my playsuits, or whatever I want, with pride.'

Not everyone was convinced about Harry's ability to call an end to toxic masculinity. 'After all, men are as capable of violence and sexism in nail polish and sequins as they are of being gentle and emotionally available in denim dungarees and steel cap boots,' wrote Madeleine Holden, for *MEL Magazine*.

She added: 'The problem is the wife beating, homophobic slur hurling and endless pissing matches, not the outfits men wear when they do these things.'

Writing for *Razz* magazine, Amy Milner agreed. She wrote: 'Overall, I disagree with the notion that floral suits on their own can "destroy toxic masculinity". I appreciate fashion because it is interesting to analyse both its aesthetics, and what it represents. Although fashion is important, what will really make a difference is in the way men treat each other, treat women, and are treated by society as a whole. A person's words and actions are far more important when it comes to positive role models in the media.'

Harry has a theory on where this all started. In an interview with Timothée Chalamet in *i–D* in November 2018, Harry credited the fact that he 'didn't grow up in a man's man world' but with his mum and sister. He told Chalamet: 'I've become a lot more content with who I am. I think there's so much masculinity in being vulnerable and allowing yourself to be feminine, and I'm very comfortable with that.'

He continued, 'Today it's easier to embrace masculinity in so many different things. I definitely find – through music, writing, talking with friends and being open – that some of the times when I feel most confident is when I'm allowing myself to be vulnerable.'

Soon, fashion just became a part of Harry's image. Just as he was spoken of as a singer and an actor, so would he be discussed as a fashion man. In a *Rolling Stone* interview, Harry's ensemble of clothes and accessories was listed: a floppy hat, pink and mint green nail polish, and a yellow patent-canvas bag with the logo 'Chateau Marmont'.

Like many fashionistas, he plays it down. 'I always love being comfortable,' he told the *Sun*. 'You should wear what makes you feel comfortable. It's a really good opportunity to have fun – it's clothes; it's not a big deal. It's a good time to express yourself and have fun with it. It's one of those things that you shouldn't take seriously. If you want to wear a pair of yellow trousers you can wear a pair of yellow trousers.' He added: 'I love an accessory as much as the next person.'

There has long been an androgyny to Harry's personal style, which is such a positive thing in these days of increasingly fluid gender identities. 'Harry's flamboyant evolution was praised by fans for his ability to blur gender boundaries, but it's also worth taking note of the ease with which he has pushed the envelope,' said *Vogue* magazine. It also remarked that his wardrobe 'has been less people-pleasing, and instead it's more pushing boundaries of what dressing for on and off the stage looks like right now'.

Soon, the big labels came calling. In 2018, Gucci announced that Harry would become the face of its tailoring campaign. The rumours began when he was spotted on set at a fish and chip shop in suburban St Albans in March 2018, prompting speculation that he was working with Gucci in a more promotional capacity. 'Harry Styles, Gucci model. It's another perfect match for the modern multi-hyphenate,' remarked *Vogue*.

Images were snapped by Glen Luchford and art-directed by Christopher Simmonds in the eagerly awaited campaign, revealed in June 2018. He is seen modelling the house's latest suiting designs by creative director Alessandro Michele in and around a local fish and chip shop in north London.

In one photograph, he wears a New Marseille jacket with an embroidered collar detail and carries a pet chicken. In another image, he casually leans against the shop window in a Gucci Heritage retro check grey three-piece suit, eating a packet of chips, accompanied by a dog. 'Be still our beating hearts,' remarked *Vogue*.

'It's time to try something new and hopefully shock and inspire in a different way,' Harry's long-time stylist told *Miss Vogue*. 'I know the fans love his outfits, so hopefully they will love what's to come.' For a while back there it seemed that what was to come was going to be a whole load of flared trousers. 'It was really fun,' Harry said of one of the first times he wore such strides. 'I just kind of started wearing more and more of it, and at the same time just becoming a lot more comfortable in myself.'

> He also donated a pair of rainbow shoes he had worn during his promotional tour for *Dunkirk* to London Friend, a charity that advocates for LGBTQ+ mental health and well-being services.

In June 2018 he released two T-shirts with his 'Treat People With Kindness' slogan designed with the colours of the Pride flag. He donated all profits to GLSEN, which works to create safe and inclusive environments in schools across the USA for LGBTQ+ youth. In a similar vein, he also donated a pair of rainbow shoes he had worn during his promotional tour for *Dunkirk* to London Friend, a charity that advocates for LGBTQ+ mental health and well-being services.

When he co-hosted the Met Gala in 2019, his outfit more than lived up to the feverish expectation. His sheer frilled black blouse and tailored trousers were the talk of the night. As *Vogue* put it, the costume 'put together references ranging from the New Romantic movement to the Victorian era, while sticking to the camp theme of the evening'.

Harry had his ears pierced especially for the night and wore a drop-pearl earring. 'It was the perfect final touch for the outfit.

'About four days ago, the day before I left to travel to New York, I was on Gucci's website and saw these pearl earrings,' Lambert said. 'Harry and I have discussed previously piercing his ears, and this was the perfect time. I texted him and he replied saying, "Let's do it."'

Lambert talked *Miss Vogue* through the unexpected look. 'I think everyone was expecting Harry to be in sequins, bright colours and a crown, but we decided on a different type of "camp" that hopefully would surprise,' he said.

'After such a colourful tour wardrobe it is nice to do something a little unexpected. This look is about taking traditionally feminine elements like the frills, heeled boots, sheer fabric

> 'Everyone was expecting Harry to be in sequins, bright colours and a crown, but we decided on a different type of "camp" that hopefully would surprise.'

and the pearl earring, but then rephrasing them as masculine pieces set against the high-waisted tailored trousers and his tattoos. The look, I feel, is elegant. It's camp, but still Harry.'

It had been a long time coming: Harry had begun speaking about it with Alessandro Michele months before the big night. 'We met up earlier this year to share mood boards with the Gucci team,' Lambert explained. 'We had pages of printed references all on the table from Alessandro, myself and Harry, then we edited them down.

'Alessandro and the design team are a dream to work with, they came back with around twenty designs,' he went on. 'Harry and myself went through all the fabrics, sketches and ideas and shared our favourites. From there, Gucci produced samples of these and fittings commenced.' Asked why he did not simply stick with the floral flares that had proved such a hit for Harry, Lambert said: 'I think we've done that chapter … This is a more subtle form of camp, which I love.'

Harry wore a different outfit for the after-party, which was hosted by Gucci on a college basketball court of all places. His after-party outfit was dominated by a red statement bow tie, a cross earring and a billowing-sleeve shirt with buttonhole details. According to Lambert, the second look was intended as an homage to the New Romantic movement that flourished primarily in eighties London.

He has also worked with smaller brands, including talents that are still emerging. 'We are very keen to work with young brands like Harris Reed, Charles Jeffrey and Palomo Spain – they have been really key in expressing Harry's style. Every time a new season of shows happens, Harry and I will go through the shows and share looks we like, acting as a springboard for what he might wear. Just recently, Harry shared references of a fashion direction he would like to try and we have just finished working on a mood board together for things to come.'

When he worked with Harris Reed, the student was full of praise for the pop star. 'The whole experience was extremely collaborative,' said the twenty-one-year-old fashionista. 'Both were very involved from the beginning in not only seeing the sketches and approving all the fabrics, but then Harry Styles really got to know me and who I was through the times we spent together.

'I made it clear from the beginning that I am someone who needs meaning to be behind everything I do and that my designs are not just clothes, but an extension of who I am and what I stand for. Harry could not have been a more lovely or supportive client throughout this entire process. He never held back if he loved something.

'I wanted the clothes to tell a story through their movement. Harry loves a good suit and he should – he looks amazing in them – but for the pieces I wanted to create, I wanted to have as much of the fabric flowing with every movement he made as possible,' the designer explained. 'Every time I design, I come up with a narrative of who that person is, what they stand for, what they do and what they want to convey to the world. Seeing Harry dancing along the stage and making it his own was the perfect ending to that story.'

* * *

Musicians getting into fashion is nothing new but the connection between the two worlds is certainly getting strong. It started with crossovers like Madonna's clothing line Material Girl but has now grown into something much bigger.

Kanye West's Yeezy brand, estimated in 2019 to be worth $1.5 billion, is an example of the riches that can be had.

Rihanna has also delved headfirst into fashion: she was creative director of women's collections for Puma, and has designed lingerie under the Savage × Fenty banner. Then she established her own *maison* with LVMH, joining the ranks of Dior, Fendi and Louis Vuitton. As *Vogue* magazine explained, you can now 'follow Rihanna on Instagram, stream her music via Spotify, dress in her Fenty tailored denim, buy her cosmetics at Harvey Nichols and sleep in her Savage × Fenty pyjamas … all bases are covered.'

Pharrell Williams became co-owner of G-Star RAW, launching an Elwood X25 denim collection, founding streetwear brand Billionaire Boys Club and tying up with Adidas. Gwen Stefani launched her L.A.M.B. brand. Demi Lovato's partnership with Kate Hudson's Fabletics athletic wear has been a hit for the gym crowd, as has Beyoncé's athletic-wear brand Ivy Park.

Then, of course, we have Victoria Beckham, who has become so ensconced in the world of fashion that she is now more associated with clothing than pop music. These are the sorts of figures who have trodden the path between pop music and fashion that Harry has now sauntered along.

In December 2019, Harry dropped a limited-edition collaboration with Gucci creative director Alessandro Michele to celebrate the release of his new album. It featured his name scrawled inside a bleeding, red heart. It was truly limited: the shirt was only on sale for one day. But it helped a good cause: a portion of the proceeds from sales benefitted the Global Fund for Women.

He promoted the T-shirt as he arrived at the BBC Radio Live Lounge in December 2019. Catching the attention as ever, he paired the shirt with a custom Bode jacket cut from an antique wool blanket and added wide-leg trousers and blue nail polish.

He sure knows how get the cameras flashing as he arrives places. When he went to the Gucci Cruise 2020 fashion show, he wore a cream-coloured suit with a ribbed tank top underneath. He added fingers full of chunky rings and pastel polishes, an oversized clutch, rose-coloured sunglasses.

> 'In typical Harry, uh, style, he added red Chelsea boots embroidered with dragons, giving him that necessary flare.'

At the 2017 premiere of *Dunkirk*, he opted for a classic black suit and white shirt. But, as *Wonderwall* wrote, 'in typical Harry, uh, style, he added red Chelsea boots embroidered with dragons, giving him that necessary flare [sic]'. The same year he also helped launch Gucci's new Mémoire d'une Odeur fragrance campaign. 'The triggering of memories from smell is really strong for everyone,' he said. 'My mother has always worn the same perfume. It smells like roman candles and jasmine. So like any time I smell it, I feel like a kid again. I feel like everyone has those.

'It transcends gender. I really like wearing it because it's [Gucci's] first universal fragrance.' He also confirmed that he actually does wear the perfume every day: 'I sleep in it.'

For anyone looking to emulate Harry's look, it is worth listening to the words of Lambert, who has shared style tips for men, saying: 'A boot looks clean with a suit, and one with a slight heel can elongate your legs.' For trousers, he said: 'I really like a loose-fit trouser. I don't find a super-skinny leg to be flattering to anyone.'

For shirts, he says: 'When dressing up, I always advise against wearing shirts that are too stiff. They look uncomfortable and don't photograph very well. A lot of shops these days offer so many different colours. Brands like Gucci, Givenchy – they have simple shirts but in great fabrics that can modernize any suit.'

The fashion world continues to recognize Harry. As he won a place in *GQ*'s '50 best dressed men of 2020', Daniel Fletcher, fashion designer and star of the hit Netflix show *Next in Fashion*, said: 'Harry's sense of style is so unique. He's fearless and I love that about him. His ability to blur gender boundaries and embrace his femininity without looking like he's thought twice about it is absolutely unparalleled.'

* * *

As well as grabbing attention for what he wears, Harry has also been known to grab attention for what he doesn't wear. We saw how as a child he enjoyed pulling his trousers down and 'mooning' people. Then, in the *X Factor* house, he chuckled at the reaction he caused when he strolled around with nothing on.

So really it was natural when, at twenty-five, the artwork for his solo record saw him strip completely naked. He is photographed closing his eyes, with one hand on his hip, while crossing his legs to hide his genitals. His feet are rested on the edge of a giant heart. Another image is a shirtless snap, featuring Harry smouldering down the lens of the lucky photographer's camera. The media went into overdrive, with the *Metro* shouting that Harry was 'all kinds of naked'.

Harry told *The Ellen DeGeneres Show* how the naked photos came into being. 'We tried it with some other stuff, and it was one of those things where he [the photographer] was like, "Okay, this shirt's not really working, so let's try it without the shirt," and then it's like, "Those trousers aren't really working, so let's try it without the trousers,'" he said, with a smile. 'And then he kind of looked at me, and I was like, "These pants aren't working, are they?"'

The naked images came despite the fact that Harry said he considered being a sex symbol a 'very strange, dynamic thing', and he also confessed to finding it 'weird' that people consider him attractive. 'Honestly, I'd say I try and think about it as little as possible,' he told Zane Lowe on Apple Music's Beats 1 Radio.

'I guess the thing with like sex, in general, is like, it used to feel so much more taboo for me,' he continued. 'Even like when we were in the band, the thought of people thinking that I had sex was like, "Oh no, that's crazy. What if they know?"'

The praise just keeps coming Harry's way. Commenting on photographs of Harry, *Esquire* magazine said: 'Styles's outfit isn't a natural fit. There are stripes. These aren't always best-placed alongside big graphic embroidery. Nor are they complementary to cords (and flares), and beaded necklaces, and a lick of red nail polish. And yet, it does work, because Styles has published his own rulebook by breaking the rules. … As designer Dries Van Noten and Gucci have long proved, they work well, especially when combined with the showmanship of Mick Jagger headlining a Vegas residency that never came to fruition.'

* * *

They started on his eighteenth birthday, when he had a black star inked onto his inner left arm. By 2020, it was estimated that he had fifty-six. We're talking tattoos. They are spread over Harry's arms and torso. They range from small letters to all-out fine-line drawings. He has a coat hanger on his arm, which many have speculated is a sign of his support for the pro-choice movement, as it's a well-known symbol of support.

Harry has been coy about the inspiration and symbolism of many of his inks. For example, when asked why he got a tattoo of a mermaid, he said: 'I am a mermaid.' Many of his tattoos are tributes to his loved ones. For instance, he has the dates '1957' and '1967' on his collarbones (his father and mother's years of birth, respectively) and the name of his godson, Jackson. His sister Gemma's name is inked on him in Hebrew. He also has an 'R' that's believed to refer to his stepfather, Robin Twist, and an 'A' to represent his mother, Anne, in the crook of his arm.

His '17 Black' inking is thought to be a reference to James Bond's lucky bet from the casino scene in *Diamonds Are Forever*. However, celebrity tattooist Kevin Paul told *GQ* it was a symbol of misfortune. 'Basically, Harry lost money gambling – I think it was in Australia – and he lost it on seventeen black. This was in the early days, the first few years of One Direction.'

He also has the word Pingu under his arm. His pal Ed Sheeran has the character Pingu among his tattoos. 'We did both Seventeen Black and Pingu on the same day,' says star inker Paul. 'He and Ed had been out the night before, got pissed and started talking about their favourite childhood shows, and *Pingu* was both of their favourites, which is why they both decided to get them.'

He has had various tattoos covered up with new ones over the years. An example of this is the large anchor on his forearm, which he got to cover an original tattoo that said, 'I can't change'. The ship tattoo on his upper left arm happened while he was reportedly dating Taylor Swift. It was inked onto him by one of his other regular tattoo artists, Freddy Negrete, at the famous LA parlour Shamrock Social Club, where other stars including Adele and Lady Gaga have visited.

Perhaps the most famous of his tattoos is the butterfly in the middle of his torso. He got this in 2013, when he was just nineteen.

On his upper arm are a giant ship, a skeleton in a suit and top hat, a rose and two hands shaking.

It was done by Liam Sparkes, who has also inked Harry's former bandmate Louis Tomlinson several times. The tattoo artist speculates that this ink was inspired by *Papillon*, the French movie that sees two men escape from prison.

Then there are the swallows that make up his other best-known tattoos. He got them in 2012. He has revealed the meaning behind these: 'I got two swallows on my chest,' Styles told *Us Weekly*. 'I like that kind of style of tattoos, like the old sailor kind of tattoos. They symbolize travelling, and we travel a lot!'

On his lower left arm, you'll find a giant heart, a liquor bottle with the words, 'you booze, you lose' and a Bible. On his upper arm are a giant ship, a skeleton in a suit and top hat, a rose and two hands shaking. Turn it round, and on his inner left bicep are the Green Bay Packers logo (he lost a bet), three nails, a coat hanger and a star. On the left he also has the word 'Jackson' written in cursive.

During an appearance on *The Late Late Show*, James Corden had the members of One Direction select random boxes, with one member getting stuck with a 'tattoo' box. It was Harry who ended up with the unlucky box and had to get the show's logo tattooed on him.

The inks just keep on coming: in tribute to his three favourite cities, Harry has 'NY', 'LA' and 'Lon' next to each other. Then there is the question, 'Can I stay?'. Those who have had a good look at the photo on the cover of his debut solo album might have noticed Harry's small tattoo of a guitar. There have been three nails hovering menacingly next to his armpit since 2013. Also thought to have been added in the summer of 2013, Harry has an ink of a cross on his left hand, near his thumb. This one has prompted comparisons with Justin Bieber, who has crucifix tattoos on his arm, chest and face.

It's safe to say that he is a fan of tattoos but then so are lots of pop stars in 2020. Adam Levine, Justin Bieber, Rihanna and Miley Cyrus are among those with many. Professor Green, Demi Levato and other former members of One Direction are also covered in ink. Louis Tomlinson even has one on his bum. Niall Horan also tried to get one on his backside but was told by the inker that his butt was 'too squidgy'. Mostly, Harry has been happy with his tattoos, though he has mixed feelings about one. 'I regret this one on my wrist here,' he told *We Love Pop*. 'There are some that my friends have done and some that are just awful.'

Many of the tattoos are near Harry's nipples – and those nipples have taken on a celebrity of their own. Right from the first moment he was seen shirtless, during judges' houses on *The X Factor*, there has been speculation over just how many nipples Harry has. It seemed he certainly had more than the usual two.

Then, in 2017, he put the matter to bed, so his fans could rest easy at night once more. During an interview with Chelsea Handler, the topic came up. 'There's a rumour on the internet that you have four nipples. Have you heard that?' she asked. Harry replied: 'Correct.' Handler said, 'You do?' and he answered again, 'Yeah.' She asked him to point them out and he did, over his shirt.

This is not as uncommon as many believe. Joshua Zeichner, MD, director of cosmetic and clinical research for the Department of Dermatology at Mount Sinai Hospital in New York, told *Allure* how it happens. 'When the body develops, sometimes nipple-forming cells accidentally migrate down the chest below the normal nipple,' he said. 'Supernumerary nipples can develop anywhere on the chest, armpit, even belly or into the groin, along a vertical line below the nipple, known as the "embryonic milk line".'

Fans have become obsessed with Harry's tattoos. So has the media. But that is not the only part of Harry's body that has attracted feverish discussion – his hair has undergone quite a transformation of its own. From the mop of his One Direction days, to the wilder look dubbed 'lionesque' by *GQ* magazine and the side-sweep look, which was more groomed but still big and striking, it's undergone many transformations.

In 2013 came the high-flying bouffant quiff: 'you can immediately sense the Hollywood star coming at this stage', commented *GQ* of this memorable look. In 2014, the Keith Richards-style headscarves joined the Harry hair party. There were bandanas and man buns. The following year he went all Mick Jagger on us, with a more shoulder-length look that coincided with his peak Gucci period.

For so long, his hair had been moving in, pardon the pun, one direction, but in 2016 it went the other way. He cut his hair shorter and prepared for Hollywood. Within

> It's an emotional issue and not every fan has been enamoured by every change along the way.

months it was shorter still, as he filmed *Dunkirk*. For some fans, this took a lot of getting used to. It's an emotional issue and not every fan has been enamoured by every change along the way.

More recently, he has started to grow his hair out again. In 2017, it was less curly than previously but in 2018, the curls were back. By the spring of 2019, he had curls at mid-length but then the curls disappeared, causing a great deal of upset. As *Allure* put it: 'Word spread rapidly among his fans – and many of them are not cool with this. While plenty have swarmed the internet to say he still looks great, others are getting very real about just how much they hate the fact that Styles's curls are gone. Twitter is basically about to throw a riot over this dude's hair.' As one Harry fan on Twitter put it: 'Whoever cut Harry Styles [sic] hair should be SACKED.'

Cosmopolitan has entered the heated debate. In December 2019, it asked the big question: 'Is Harry Styles Hotter With Long Hair or Short Hair?' An online poll alongside the article found that 71 per cent found Harry better with short hair, against 29 per cent preferring him with long hair. The man himself went along with this thinking. 'I was, like, the one with the long hair,' he said. 'I'd had it for so much of One Direction. Cutting it off just felt very much like starting afresh.'

For Harry, his appearance is just another way of communicating with the world. Whether it's through his clothes, accessories, tattoos or even his hair. Many feel he communicates just as well with his clothes as he does the words of his songs. As *GQ* said: 'Designers who have worked with him, as well as fashion chroniclers, praise his ability to communicate through clothing.'

CHAPTER NINE

LOVE LIFE

As far as the media was concerned, it was a romance made in heaven: a beautiful, blond singer with a history of heartbreak, and a handsomely cute boy-band member. Between them, the two had many millions of fans around the world who followed their every move. No wonder their reported fling generated many miles of column inches. Indeed, the connection between Harry and Taylor Swift was so convenient that the question was asked over how deep their relationship really was.

For a long time, the media had tried to link him to a chain of people. Most of the stories were fabricated. There was even speculation that the Radio 1 host Nick Grimshaw, a close friend of Harry's, was romantically involved with the young singer, something they both deny. Then there was the speculation that Harry was involved with bandmate Louis Tomlinson, which we will return to.

At one point, Harry was moved to say he felt as if he had '7,000 girlfriends' – according to the media, at least. As for Swift, she too had massive media currency. There were few celebrity magazine editors who did not covet juicy gossip involving her. So when whispers began to circulate that the two had become an item, it was bound to be a big story.

It was reported that the pair met for the first time at an awards night in 2012. It was March and the Nickelodeon Kids' Choice Awards was in full swing. Swift was spied dancing during One Direction's performance. The press present sensed the opportunity for a story. Later, after the two singers had chatted, Styles was asked if he had anything to report. With a smile, he described Taylor as 'nice'.

Justin Bieber then stoked the speculation when he teased the media with a deliberately cryptic allusion to the presumed couple. He said: 'I already know one of the biggest artists in the world thinks Harry is so hot but I have been sworn to secrecy.' Harry's One Direction bandmates were also seen several times teasing him about the gossip, including at the MTV Video Music Awards.

> 'I already know one of the biggest artists in the world thinks Harry is so hot but I have been sworn to secrecy.'

When Swift appeared at the final of *The X Factor*, the show's presenter Mario Lopez offered the press what he called 'a little inside scoop'. He said: 'During the rehearsals, Harry from One Direction came and slapped me on the back, and said: "Hey Mario, how ya doing?" And I said, "What are you doing here?" And he sort of pointed toward Taylor.' Lopez said they left holding hands. The show's official Twitter feed also bumped up the story, saying the two had eaten cheeseburgers together.

Yet still nothing had been officially confirmed. Swift was seen wearing a silver aeroplane chain identical to one owned by Styles.

She also hinted that she was now interested in relationships with bad boys. She added: 'There's a really interesting charisma involved. They usually have a lot to say, and even if they don't, they know how to look at you to say it all. I think every girl's dream is to find a bad boy at the right time, when he wants to not be bad any more.'

Harry's close friend Grimshaw was the first to confirm the relationship. 'Harry really likes Taylor, he's fallen for her in a big way,' he said. 'At first, I wasn't sure if the relationship was a real one but I talk to him a lot and it seems to be that she's the one for him – for now, anyway.'

The disc jockey added: 'Harry likes people who make him laugh. I talk to Harry a lot on the phone while he's away touring and he talks about her a lot. He is very happy with her.'

Naturally, these quotes were very popular in the media, but what the magazines and newspapers wanted were photographs. They finally got the snaps when Taylor and Harry visited Central Park Zoo together. After that date, the two reportedly spent two evenings together at Swift's hotel in Manhattan. Then they were seen at the after-party of a 1D gig at Madison Square Garden. They left at 4 a.m. and retired to the same hotel, then emerged the next morning.

In the new year, they were spotted together in Britain. They ate at the George & Dragon in Great Budworth, Cheshire. 'He's amazing,' Taylor was reported to have said of Harry. They also went for a walk in the Peak District and dined with Styles's sister at the Rising Sun. Harry reportedly introduced Taylor to the goofy UK teen comedy *The Inbetweeners* while she was in Britain. Apparently she loved it.

Naturally, various celeb magazines competed to make the story into a bigger and bigger deal. Unnamed 'insiders' were telling the press that Harry and Swift were planning to marry. It was at this stage that, according to reports, Swift's father intervened and took Harry to one side to tell him to 'slow down and take things easy'. While Father Swift was, according to the reports, not seeking to split the couple up, he was arguing strongly that they should not rush into anything.

Early in 2013 Taylor and Harry jetted to the British Virgin Islands. Photographs were snapped of them eating alongside some fans at a restaurant in Virgin Gorda. It all looked blissful but later the same day, Swift was spotted alone and looking sad on a boat, while Harry continued to party elsewhere. The media took this as a sign the couple had broken up. It has been alleged that they had had a big row, during which Swift had told Harry he was 'lucky' to be with her.

Much of the reporting over what went wrong had been speculation and then the speculation turned to whether there had in fact been a relationship in the first place. The American tabloid *National Enquirer* said of Swift: 'Little does Taylor know that Harry's handlers went to great lengths to put the two together because she's such a huge star.'

> It has since been claimed that Taylor's big hit 'I Knew You Were Trouble' is about Harry. This theory was bolstered when Taylor discussed performing the song at the BRIT Awards.

The *Guardian* said sourly that it was 'inevitable' that they would have dated 'seeing as, between them, they have allegedly dated every single person on the planet'. With cynicism to the fore, it added that 'the fact this relationship happened to bookend Swift releasing an album and One Direction announcing a tour is just one of those coincidences that often accompanies celebrity relationships'. In case readers had not understood the implication, it added that 'some of their dates might have had the suspicious smack of PR exercises'.

It has since been claimed that Taylor's big hit 'I Knew You Were Trouble' is about Harry. This theory was bolstered when Taylor discussed performing the song at the BRIT Awards, a ceremony at which Harry was present. 'Well, it's not hard to access that emotion when the person the song is directed at is standing by the side of the stage watching,' she said.

However, a more cynical examination suggests that the Harry link was just being fabricated to boost publicity. The song was previewed in early autumn of 2012 but Swift had been working on the album it appeared on, *Red*, for nearly two years before that. In all, she wrote thirty songs for *Red*, of which around half made the final cut. Generally, the songwriting for a major-release album is completed many months ahead of its release, or sometimes as much as a year or more.

The theory that her song 'Style', which appears on *1989*, is about Harry holds more water. 'Out of the Woods' is also thought to be about him. Indeed, according to *Spin*, it is not the only song about him on that album. 'Many of the songs on *1989* seem to be about Styles, whether literally or contextually: He was her only public relationship between the release of *Red* and *1989*,' it says.

It is also theorized that Harry co-wrote the song 'Perfect' about Swift. The lyrics, addressed to someone who 'likes writing break-up songs', certainly seem to be aimed at Swift. Asked by *People* whether it was about her, he said: 'I'm never going to tell someone what a song's about because I feel like it's up to them.'

More recently, Harry has spoken less cattily of Swift and of her tendency to write break-up songs. 'Certain things don't work out. There's a lot of things that can be right, and it's still wrong,' he told *Rolling Stone*. 'In writing songs about stuff like that, I like tipping a hat to the time together. You're celebrating the fact it was powerful and made you feel something, rather than "this didn't work out, and that's bad". And if you run into that person, maybe it's awkward, maybe you have to get drunk ... but you shared something. Meeting someone new, sharing those experiences, it's the best s--t ever. So thank you.'

Harry said that he doesn't actually know if the songs are about him or not, but he said, 'the issue is, she's so good, they're bloody everywhere'.

Warming to his theme, he added: 'I'm lucky if everything [we went through] helped create those songs. That's what hits your heart. That's the stuff that's hardest to say, and it's the stuff I talk least about. That's the part that's about the two people. I'm never going to tell anybody everything.'

Movingly, he also looked back over the day he and Swift walked in Central Park, and how he feels when he sees the widely published photographs of it. 'When I see photos from that day,' he says, 'I think: Relationships are hard, at any age. And adding in that you don't really understand exactly how it works when you're eighteen, trying to navigate all that stuff didn't make it easier. I mean, you're a little bit awkward to begin with. You're on a date with someone you really like. It should be that simple, right? It was a learning experience for sure. But at the heart of it – I just wanted it to be a normal date.'

* * *

The moment he stepped onto the stage for his first X Factor audition, Harry left behind his chances of ever having a truly normal date again. However, he simultaneously increased his chances of having a date. Indeed, since he has become famous he has been linked to a host of glamorous women.

In the summer of 2012, rumours circulated that he was having a relationship with Lucy Horobin, a radio DJ. She was thirty-one, a similar age gap between the two as there had been between Harry and Caroline Flack.

According to reports, the attraction began when Horobin interviewed One Direction for her Manchester radio station. Harry and Horobin flirted on air, as Harry told the host she 'looked lovely'.

She was going through a rough patch with her husband, Oliver, at the time. He has since gone to the papers to speak of how upset he was by what happened between the pair. 'The moment I discovered Harry had slept with my wife still haunts me,' he told the *Mirror*. 'Knowing they slept together and then Lucy came back home and climbed into bed with me hurts the most.

'Realizing my wife had decided to leave me because she had fallen for a seventeen-year-old boy, that's the most embarrassing thing. I'm a man in my thirties and she left me for him, a young lad. That's what has ripped me of my dignity.' Harry has since insisted that she had separated from her husband at the time and he had no idea she was still married.

Oliver, though, was in no mood to forgive and forget as he spoke to the press. 'I know how stupid it sounds but I blame Harry one hundred per cent for this,' he said.

'Okay, so Lucy may have technically split from me days before he first slept with her but that came after weeks of flirtatious text messages. We were still living together in the same house. At that point, in the same bed. She was wearing a wedding ring the first time they met. I don't think it matters to him whether the woman he wants is married or not.'

As we saw earlier, Emma Ostilly had followed the example of Caroline Flack and deleted her social media accounts in the face of abuse from Harry's fans when it was reported he was seeing her. It was said that he had dumped Taylor Swift for Ostilly.

The American model appeared in the video for One Direction's second single, 'It's Gotta Be You'. Unlike some of Harry's other lovers, Ostilly is the same age as Harry and they were both eighteen when they met. Soon after they first set eyes upon each other, he visited her at her New Zealand home.

An eyewitness who saw the couple together in a bar said: 'They really seemed to have a connection and only had eyes for each other. They were enjoying themselves, laughing and joking together. They seemed very happy and relaxed and you could tell they have a history together.'

Asked about the nature of their relationship, Harry said: 'She's just a friend … I prefer not to talk about it.' However, that was not enough to spare her from the social media wrath of angry One Direction fans. Members of the 1D army soon forced the eighteen-year-old to quit Twitter. This caused much amusement to those fans who had been horrid to her. 'Emma Ostilly deleted her twitter … HAHAHAHAHAAHAHAHA WHY AM I LAUGHING SO HARD,' tweeted one.

Emily Atack was an actress from *The Inbetweeners* who reportedly enjoyed some steamy liaisons with Harry during 2012. She had actually been an admirer of Harry since his run on *The X Factor* in 2010. She tweeted: 'Does Harry from One Direction HAVE to be 16?! Let's pretend he's 18 at least! Then there'd be only One Direction he'd be going – to the bedroom!'

It seemed they did just that. She later told *Reveal*: 'Yeah, we had a short-lived thing. But we were never boyfriend and girlfriend. Harry and I had fun, then went in opposite directions. We haven't spoken in a while.'

> Like several other women, she learned that many of Harry's fans could be vicious to anyone linked to their hero.

Like several other women, she learned that many of Harry's fans could be vicious to anyone linked to their hero. 'I learned that, with Twitter, you maybe have to think before you tweet,' she said. 'I've made up my mind never to say anything about Harry again.'

Caggie Dunlop was a star of the TV show *Made in Chelsea*. She was linked with Harry during 2012. That year, a source told the *Sunday Mirror*: 'She and Harry have been in touch for around a year, but they first kissed about nine months ago. Things went cold for a while, but they hooked up on Thursday night and ended up spending the night together.'

They were spotted leaving a nightclub, before speeding off towards Chelsea Harbour in Harry's £50,000 Range Rover Sport. A source said the pair had 'obviously real chemistry between them' but the two insisted that nothing but friendship exists between them. A friend of Dunlop's spoke about the impact that the sudden surge in attention had on the actress. 'It was horrible for Caggie,' said Millie Mackintosh, in an interview with *Marie Claire*. 'I'm not going to speak about it, but when people are showing up outside your parents' house it's gone too far.'

However, she did add: 'Caggie is a fun-loving girl, I don't think she minded the attention too much but it does all get a bit much. There's a different direction she wanted to go in and I think she got a bit freaked out.'

Kimberly Stewart – the daughter of controversial rocker Rod Stewart – has also been linked with Harry. It all seemed to happen when Harry went out for dinner with the family. As Rod himself cheekily revealed to Alan Carr on *Chatty Man*: 'His car was here in the morning, let's put it that way. But he may just have come round to pick something up … I've let the cat out of the bag. Harry couldn't be kinder. He is a very funny guy.'

When Harry was photographed kissing US model Paige Reifler in 2014, she told the *Mirror*: 'Yes, I am seeing him.' One Harry fan took it upon herself on Twitter to interrogate and threaten Reifler. 'Are you dating Harry or not,' she tweeted. 'That's the only thing we want to know and when we don't get answers we kill.'

As we have seen, it is rumoured that Harry's first solo album is largely about the on–off relationship he had with Kendall Jenner, the American model and media personality best known for her role in the reality television show *Keeping Up With the Kardashians*.

The rumoured fling began in 2014, when they were spotted

looking 'very cute' and 'flirting' in California. The following year, they were snapped on vacation in Anguilla and St Barts. Then Jenner's sister, Khloe Kardashian, told *Entertainment Tonight*: 'Do I think they're dating? Yes. I don't know if they're like boyfriend–girlfriend.

'Nowadays, I don't know, people are weird with stuff. So I don't know their "title". But, I mean, they were in St Barts together, hanging out, so to me that's dating. I would call that dating.' Although they have since stopped dating, they have been spotted together again. After the 2020 BRIT Awards, Harry was snapped chatting with Jenner at the Standard Hotel in London in the early hours of the following morning.

The list of other women Harry has been linked to over the years of his celebrity is very long. There have been unconfirmed rumours of him dating Victoria's Secret model Nadine Leopold, *X Factor* judge/Pussycat Doll Nicole Scherzinger and chef Tess Ward. How many of these rumoured flings were real is open to debate and speculation.

* * *

Perhaps the most explosive rumoured relationship was not with a woman but a man – none other than Harry's former bandmate Louis Tomlinson.

Right from the early days of One Direction, there were wild internet rumours that the two band members were an item. There were Tumblr accounts dedicated to their supposed relationship, with graphic erotic fan fiction. Videos of the band onstage or giving interviews were pored over for evidence. The theory even conjured a 'couple name' for the two men: 'Stylinson'.

No amount of counter-evidence could put the theorists off their trail. In fact, any evidence to the contrary was merely twisted as proof of their theory. For instance, when Louis became a father, the Stylinson shippers said the baby was either given birth to by a surrogate mum and was in fact Louis and Harry's child, or it was a doll.

Tomlinson has spoken with both weariness and anger on the matter. 'It created this atmosphere between the two of us where everyone was looking into everything we did,' he said. 'It took away the vibe you get off anyone. It made everything, I think on both fences, a little bit more unapproachable.'

In a separate interview, he said. 'I know, culturally, it's interesting, but I'm just a bit tired of it.' When HBO drama *Euphoria* showed an animated sequence of Tomlinson and Styles in flagrante, for Louis this was the final straw.

'Again, I get the cultural intention behind that,' he said. 'It just felt a little bit … No, I'm not going to lie, I was pissed off. It annoyed me that a big company would get behind it.'

Speaking to a *Sun* podcast, he added: 'But in the end it's so far-fetched that it's just like I don't even know what to say about it, you know what I mean? It's like, "You believe that?" It's a little bit worrying. Makes me question other conspiracies that I've bought into in the past.'

Malik has also denied the rumours about Harry and Tomlinson. The former 1D member also said the gossip put a strain on the pair. 'It's not funny, and it still continues to be quite hard for them,' he said. 'They won't naturally go put their arm around each other because they're conscious of this thing that's going on, which is not even true.'

Harry has never spoken in any depth about the rumours of a relationship with Tomlinson. However, when there was speculation that the subject of his song 'Sweet Creature' was Tomlinson, he said: 'I think if you really listen to the lyrics I think you can work out if it's really about that or not, and I would lean towards no.'

CHAPTER TEN

RICHES

Harry's success both with One Direction and beyond has come with a toll. He has had to grow up in the public eye, in the face of colossal pressure and scrutiny. He has had to work hard. In the same years that he might otherwise have been enjoying a student lifestyle, sleeping late, having laughs down the pub and slowly finding his identity under the protective wing of higher education, he has instead been sweating it out and having suggested identities perpetually thrown at him by a world that scarcely knows the real thing.

However, just as his fame has come with a toll, it has also come with a price – in the shape of a very, very healthy pay-off.

To say that One Direction were a major money-spinner won't be news to anyone. For instance, between June 2014 and June 2015 alone, One Direction earned a whopping great $130 million. In 2017, it was reported that Harry and the other members of the band each sold ten shares in their company 1D Media for £70,131,909

In 2017 it was claimed that Harry, then twenty-three years of age, was the richest of the five, with a worth of £56 million.

according to records filed with Companies House, meaning they've each trousered £14,026,381.

In 2017 it was claimed that Harry, then twenty-three years of age, was the richest of the five, with a worth of £56 million. The success of his projects since One Direction has only made him wealthier. In 2019, he came in at number three in *Heat* magazine's Celebrity Rich List with an estimated personal fortune of £64 million. He came behind Ed Sheeran, who topped the list as Britain's wealthiest star aged thirty and under with an estimated worth of £170 million. The *Harry Potter* actor Daniel Radcliffe took second place in *Heat*'s list with an estimated wealth of £90 million.

As for our Harry, the success of his solo career was felt as he beat his former bandmates Niall, Louis, Liam and Zayn, who took fifth, seventh, eighth and tenth place, respectively. Niall Horan was the second richest member of One Direction and fifth on the overall list, with a fortune standing at £49 million. Next among the 1Ders came Louis Tomlinson, with a £44-million total worth. Liam Payne was sixth on the list with a growing fortune of £42 million, while Zayn was last in line with his wealth of £36 million.

Again, Harry had proven himself to be the standout member of the band. His estimated worth was not far off double what Zayn had. Not only that, from the outside it looked as if cool Harry had tried less than his bandmates. While they often seemed to be on the hamster wheel of celebrity, breathlessly trying to keep the whole thing moving, Harry was a more distant figure in showbusiness land.

To put the rich list positions and figures in context, Sam Smith (with £32 million) and Rita Ora (£18 million) also appeared in the top 10.

With a wealth of £16 million, Stormzy made his first appearance on the list. These were other artists who Harry was outstripping.

How did he gather such a vast fortune? The Sunday Times Rich List said box-office receipts at his live shows in 2017 were £46.9 million. Net assets at his company, Erskine Records, soared by more than £12 million in 2017–18. Two separate companies show assets of £4.7 million. Therefore, the paper raised him to £58 million. As Cosmopolitan's Mehera Bonner wrote: 'Harry Styles's Net Worth Legit Just Made Me Burst Out Crying,' adding: 'To be clear: He definitely has more money than me.'

His net worth is boosted by a range of ventures including his role in Dunkirk, as well as his fashion projects. The continued sales of his solo albums, songwriting royalties, his executive producer role on the sitcom Happy Together and the riches gathered from his eighty-nine tour dates has also helped fill up the coffers.

Then, there is all the money he made during his One Direction years. Any selection of stats on what the band made is shocking. For instance, the band made $13.5 million in digital singles. Their 2014 Where We Are tour was the highest-grossing tour of the year, making $290.2 million. Meanwhile, 2013's Take Me Home tour made $114 million, and 2015's On the Road Again tour made $208 million. Then there are the films the band made. For instance, This Is Us earned a whopping $8.9 million on its opening day alone.

And let's not forget all the merchandising and sponsorship deals the band struck. Clearly, all this revenue had to be shared among not just the members of the band, but their teams and management. However, if you add up all the cash the band generated, even a modest slice of that is going to be beyond life-changing.

The Harry Styles brand has become a valuable and powerful beast. As well as feeding off it himself, he has also lent that value of his influence to a clutch of good causes. When Harry shines the spotlight of his celebrity onto an issue, potentially millions of young fans sit up and take notice.

Of course, it is hardly unknown for pop stars and other modern celebrities to collaborate with charities and other causes. Stars are often to be heard speaking of a 'cause that is close to my heart'. The cynical have often suspected that many of these moments are simply another way of getting attention and remaining in the spotlight.

However, Harry has managed to project an image of sincerity onto all of his efforts. This is partly because he has been willing to take on causes that are divisive and one that involved taking on a powerful brand. The other reason why his efforts have tended to have the ring of sincerity to them is his selectiveness: rather than hopping into bed with causes left, right and centre, he has been choosy about who he supports. There is a good reason for this, as we shall see.

In 2012, he supported the young people's cancer charity Trekstock, but Harry's style of philanthropy really began in 2015, midway through a One Direction show in San Diego. During inter-song banter, he asked the audience: 'Does anybody like dolphins?' After the crowd responded, 'Yes,' he told them: 'Don't go to SeaWorld.'

The US theme park had become embroiled in controversy when, in 2013, its treatment of killer whales in captivity was the basis of the movie *Blackfish*, which documents the history of Tilikum, a killer whale captured by SeaLand of the Pacific and later transported to SeaWorld Orlando.

Harry's concert comment was caught on the phones of hundreds of fans, including the *Game of Thrones* actress Maisie Williams. They began to share what he had said with their friends. Williams shared it with her 1.2 million followers with the caption: 'You heard him ladies and gents. Don't go to SeaWorld.'

Naturally, Harry's sentiment went viral on social media and it was here that the sheer scale of his influence became clear. The investment bank Credit Suisse said there was a huge spike in online mentions of SeaWorld and a surge of negative commentary.

SeaWorld naturally tried to scramble back their reputation, as they saw the reach of Harry's denouncement of them. The company posted a message that said: 'Dear Harry, we've seen a concert clip of you urging your fans not to visit SeaWorld. We want you to know we love dolphins too. We care for the animals in our parks like we would our own family.

'We are committed to making sure their lives are enriching and they are continually engaged socially, mentally and physically. And, we also care for animals in the wild. We invite you to see for yourself, and then decide based on facts.'

But for many fans this was simply too late: Harry had turned their heads and opened their eyes to the realities of animal captors. SeaWorld Entertainment duly reported an 84 per cent drop in earnings and a two per cent drop in visitor numbers. Harry had spoken and the world had listened.

There have since been rumours that Harry has gone vegan. His association with the plant-based lifestyle began in 2018, when he was praised by his fans for using a vegan pie as part of an onstage prank.

It began when he 'pied' support act Mabel McVey in the face following their final performance together in Dublin. McVey found the prank amusing and, taking to Twitter afterwards, she wrote: 'At least [the pie] was vegan.'

Harry got praised for this. One of Mabel's fans on the micro-blogging website replied: 'Literally, how can you be so damn respectful that you ensure you throw a vegan cream pie at a vegan?' Another wrote: 'Exactly, my little vegan heart just melted!'

During his hosting gig on *Saturday Night Live* in 2020, Aidy Bryant fed Harry ham. 'He was so game,' she said. 'And right away when he got to set, we were like, "You need to get on all fours, and I'm gonna dangle this garbage in your mouth." And he was, like, totally down.'

However, as she later revealed during a radio interview, it was in fact vegan ham that she fed him. Asked if this was his request, she told them: 'Yeah, he's vegan.' Although Harry has yet to confirm this is true, his compassion for animals has often been noted and he has long seemed to be treading towards a plant-based path.

The year after his SeaWorld statement, he made an iconic intervention in a different issue when he donated his hair to a good cause. Harry shared a photo of his chopped-off braid and hashtagged #littleprincesstrust – an organization that provides real hair wigs to children across the UK and Ireland who have lost their own hair through the rigours of cancer treatment. A wonderful cause for Harry to support.

Again, the effect was objectively huge: according to the charity's site, Harry's post caused their Facebook and Twitter followers to go up exponentially, and people around the world pledged donations after learning about his generous gesture. The transformation these causes enjoy when Harry gets involved is huge and entirely positive.

This was not the last time he supported the Little Princess Trust. After his concert to celebrate the release of his new album in 2017, at The Garage in north London, he donated the profits to the same charity. The takings from his equivalent show in the US – at LA's Troubadour theatre – went to the LA charity Safe Place for Youth. This charity describes its mission as to 'inspire, nurture, and empower the resilient human spirit of homeless youth by providing immediate and lasting solutions, one young person at a time'. (As we shall see, Harry has a big heart when it comes to the homeless, and on one occasion this landed him in trouble.)

> His compassion for animals has often been noted and he has long seemed to be treading towards a plant-based path.

Later that year, he joined Pink, Lorde and Sam Smith in the line-up for the Stand Up to Cancer concert at the Hollywood Bowl. Wearing a red suit, he sang 'Sign of the Times', 'Two Ghosts', 'Only

Angel' and 'Kiwi'. *Variety* said he had 'take-me-seriously moments' during his set. He also sang a rocked-up version of the One Direction debut hit, 'What Makes You Beautiful', which he dedicated to his mother for her fiftieth birthday.

During the concert, there was an uncomfortable moment when a fan seemed to grope him. As he sang 'Kiwi', he appeared to move a fan's hand away from his crotch area before continuing his set. His fans were horrified: some described the incident as a 'sexual assault'. There were many calls for more respect for Harry. #RespectHarry trended on Twitter after video clips of the moment appeared online.

In 2017, he also spoke movingly about the terror attack in Manchester that year while performing a show in the city's arena, in a tribute to those who died there. 'I thank you so much for being with me here tonight,' he told the crowd. 'I grew up coming to my first concerts in this room. I love this room. And I thank you for spending some time with us.'

He then introduced a song he had written for Ariana Grande. 'The next song I'm gonna play for you I wrote a few years ago and I gave it to a singer called Ariana Grande,' he said. 'She sang it a few times and now we're gonna do our version for you and if you can find some way to join in please do so. I stand with you, Manchester.'

* * *

As well as putting a healthy dent in the profits of SeaWorld, Harry has helped inject more funds into the coffers of good causes. When the cash was counted for his ambitious first solo tour, a nice slice of it was being counted by charities. The tour raised $1.2 million in charity donations (via ticket contributions, Live Nation contributions and matching payments) across sixty-two charities around the world. Harry was also credited with registering hundreds of new voters via Headcount, which has registered over 600,000 voters at concerts, music festivals and online since 2004.

It had been a very philanthropic tour, by all accounts. *Variety* says the concerts made a 'major effort for water conservation' that saved the equivalent of 10,000 single-use water bottles by fans and 3,200 by the band and crew and recycled more than 6,500 gallons of water from buses, offices, dressing rooms and other backstage areas. It also says that the influence of all this led to 5,000 direct connections between fans and the local charities. All of this was a wonderful ethos to build into the tour and made it a more positive experience for everyone concerned – classic Harry.

> Later, he decorated his guitar with a new sticker that read 'Black Lives Matter' at a show in Detroit.

Then it was time for him to return to more controversial and courageous causes. In 2018, he sported a sticker that read 'End gun violence' on his guitar during a show in Dallas. To maximize the attention given to the message, he also posted a photo of himself and his guitar to his Instagram account, captioned with 'Dallas, Live on Tour.' His gesture came after a shooting massacre at Santa Fe High School in the state. Later, he decorated his guitar with a new sticker that read 'Black Lives Matter' at a show in Detroit in June.

Although both statements will seem reasonable to many, in America the gun issue is one that is hugely divisive and contentious. The same can be said of the Black Lives Matter movement, which has caused enormous debate and raised emotions. Therefore, both issues are ones that a lesser character than Harry would run a million miles from involving themselves in.

Another cause he has added his name to was the March For Our Lives gathering, in Washington, D.C., demanding stricter gun control in the wake of the Valentine's Day mass shooting at Marjory Stoneman Douglas High School in Parkland, Florida. He tweeted that he signed the march's accompanying petition, and was encouraging fans to do the same: 'I just signed the @AMarch4OurLives petition, and you should too. H'. Other pop stars involved with promoting the march included Hayley Williams, Justin Bieber, Fifth Harmony's Lauren Jauregui and St. Vincent.

There are many more causes that Harry could have drawn attention to but he says there is a very specific reason why he has not backed more of them. He has also hinted that he dreams of one day finding the one defining cause that he can make his and focus on with the full force of his compassion and celebrity.

> He wanted to focus on a few issues so he could put his full weight behind them because he wanted to avoid 'dilution'.

Asked by the *Guardian* why he doesn't use his influence more, Harry explained that he wanted to focus on a few issues so he could put his full weight behind them because he wanted to avoid 'dilution'.

'Because I'd prefer, when I say something, for people to think I mean it. To be honest, I'm still searching for that one thing, y'know. Something I can really stand up for, and get behind, and be like: This Is My Life Fight. There's a power to doing the one thing. You want your whole weight behind it.'

When he finds that 'one thing,' he could become quite a gift to those behind it. Harry has shown the charisma, artistry and astuteness to become a very powerful and lucrative philanthropist.

CHAPTER ELEVEN

FINE LINE

No sooner had Harry reinvented himself for his first solo album than he put a new twist on matters for its follow-up. Here he would have new challenges, as it is one of the received wisdoms of the music industry that any act's second album is a tricky proposition. It is known as the difficult second album syndrome.

But for Harry, he was ready to take the bull by the horns and see what magic he could come up with. 'I think if you stay in that safe space all the time, it's very easy to get bored,' he said in *i-D* magazine. 'It's important to rip it up and start again sometimes.'

When he was in the studio working on his new album, he kept returning to a video he had stored on his phone. It was a clip of David Bowie, taken from an interview he gave in the 1990s. 'Never play to the gallery,' Bowie says in the footage. 'Never work for other people in what you do.' Harry watched and rewatched that video often. He hoped both the sentiment itself and the man who uttered it could influence his second solo outing.

He said he felt he was up against a lot of pressure to do just what Bowie had counselled against in that video: playing to the gallery by producing a broad, commercial album. 'I felt a lot of pressure to be making these big songs,' he said.

With a degree of distance from his solo debut, Harry could spot where he had bowed to that pressure. 'When I listen to the first album now, I can hear all of the places where I feel like I was playing it safe, because I just didn't want to get it wrong,' he told *Rolling Stone*.

He was also keen to eclipse everything he had done before. 'A lot of the time, when you do something that goes well, your thoughts immediately turn to "what's next?"' he has said. 'Everything moves so fast that you often don't get a chance to stop and think, "holy shit, that was really amazing".'

However, it was collaborator and producer Tyler Johnson who set him onto a different path and gave him the confidence to try to stay true to Bowie's vision. He told Harry: 'You just have to make the record that you want to make right now.'

> 'Everything moves so fast that you often don't get a chance to stop and think, "holy shit, that was really amazing".'

His producer, Johnson, has worked with some other big names, Sam Smith, Cam and Meghan Trainor among them. He grew up in Steamboat Springs, Colorado. At school he was considered something of a musical prodigy. He went on to study music, law and philosophy.

Harry has long been a Bowie disciple, so it is natural that he tried to embrace the rock icon's philosophies. When he interviewed Timothée Chalamet for *i-D*, Harry quoted the rock star as saying: 'Creativity is like wading out into the ocean. You wade out to the point where you can't touch the bottom, you're a little scared, and that's where you do your best work. But I guess a big part of going into this album was I spent a lot of time thinking about the whole process of, you make an album, and then you put it out … and then you tour it. I kind of went into the second one feeling like I want to work out how to make all of this feel really fun.'

'I am not going to lie. I was pretty surprised to see the whole mushroom thing with Harry. I always used to get told off for smoking joints.'

Some of the album was recorded at the Real World Studios in Wiltshire, England, but it was at Malibu's Shangri-La studios that a more colourful incident occurred. 'Did a lot of mushrooms in here,' he told Rolling Stone of his experiences while recording.

Expanding on this dimension of his recording process, he said: 'We'd do mushrooms, lie down on the grass and listen to Paul McCartney's Ram in the sunshine. We'd just turn the speakers into the yard,' he explained.

'This is where I was standing when we were doing mushrooms and I bit off the tip of my tongue. So I was trying to sing with all this blood gushing out of my mouth. So many fond memories, this place.'

GQ magazine said that Harry 'wrote a lot of the album while high on magic mushrooms'. The revelation drew a seemingly catty response from former 1D bandmate Louis Tomlinson, who said: 'I am not going to lie. I was pretty surprised to see the whole mushroom thing with Harry. I always used to get told off for smoking joints. But anyway … there are some people who want to be known as that guy – wild, crazy, whatever … there are some people that just are.'

Wild and crazy or not, by the summer of 2019, Harry was putting his finishing touches to the album. He summed up the songs in an interview with *Rolling Stone* magazine. 'It's all about having sex and feeling sad,' he said.

Despite that theme of sadness, Harry had really enjoyed the creation and recording of the work. 'I definitely had more fun,' he told the *Graham Norton Show*. 'I think with the first one I was, like, trying so hard not to get it wrong. I had a lot more fun making this one. I felt a lot more free.' With each passing project, Harry was feeling more and more liberated from the straitjacket that *The X Factor* and One Direction had bound him in.

It was similar to the team that had worked with Harry on his previous album. Tyler Johnson either produced or co-wrote on nearly all the tracks; Jeff Bhasker and Kid Harpoon were there too. Of this magical team, Harry said: 'If you're going in with session writers or something, you spend one or two days there, and there is no way that person really cares about your album as much as you do. Because they're into something else tomorrow. I know that Mitch, Tyler, Tom, Sammy [Witte], Jeff [Bhasker] wanted the album to be as good as I wanted it to be. They don't care if it's their song or not. They're not concerned how many songs they get on an album. They want it to be the best album it can possibly be. We'll bond over music we love and things we're going through. It's not like there's one person in the group that's like, "Well, no, I don't talk about that. I just make beats."'

So, what are the songs like individually? 'I would love people to listen to the whole album,' said Harry. 'I want people to listen to every song. Even with streaming and playlists, I love listening to records top to bottom. So I want to make albums that I want to listen to top to bottom, because that's just how I listen to music.' So let's go through every track.

He knew right away that 'Golden', a brash, 1970s soft-rock beauty, would be the natural opener for the album. He says his happiest memory of creating the album is writing the feel-good track on his second day in Shangri-La.

'When we wrote "Golden", we were sitting around the kitchen in the studio, and I was playing it on guitar,' he told *Rolling Stone*. 'There were five of us singing the harmonies – the acoustics in the kitchen made it sound so cool, so we thought, this song's gonna work.'

Speaking to *Billboard,* he took up the story. 'Immediately, as soon as we'd done it, it was like, "Oh, this is track one,"' he said. 'It's so good. I used to drive from here to the studio and listen to it. "Golden" was the perfect Pacific Coast Highway song. It feels so Malibu to me.' *Nerds and Beyond* noted that there's a 'major Fleetwood Mac influence on this track'.

'Watermelon Sugar' is a winner already just from its title – and the track does not let us down. Described as a 'fruit-crazed jam' by *Rolling Stone*, it is as tasty as you'd hope. He co-wrote it with Tyler Johnson, Tom Hull and Mitch Rowland. This is the 'Kiwi' of album two. Harry has refused to confirm or deny whether the song is about 'the joys of mutually appreciated oral pleasure', as Zane Lowe memorably put it. Nevertheless, *NOW* magazine says the song is 'sexual, grown-ass and tender'.

'Adore You' is the most poppy and upbeat song on the album – and possibly of his solo career to date. He says he found the confidence to pen such a fluffy tune from the acceptance he found during his first solo tour, and from studying the form of his musical heroes.

'This time I really felt so much less afraid to write fun pop songs,'

> 'There were five of us singing the harmonies – the acoustics in the kitchen made it sound so cool, so we thought, this song's gonna work.'

he told *Rolling Stone*. 'I listen to stuff like Harry Nilsson and Paul Simon and Van Morrison, and I think, well, Van Morrison has "Brown Eyed Girl" and Nilsson has "Coconut". Bowie has "Let's Dance". The fun stuff is important.' It was one of the final songs he wrote for the album. Perhaps his confidence in the pop tune was too much for some. For instance, the *NME* describes it as 'generic chart fodder'.

With 'Lights Up', we again see the change in mood between Harry's first two solo works. For the lead single for his debut album, he chose the epic and dark ballad 'Sign of the Times'. For the follow-up, he chose this short, upbeat R&B song.

'When I played it for the label, I told them, "This is the first single. It's two minutes, thirty-five. You're welcome,"' he recalled to *Rolling Stone*. He also remembers when he learned that his granddad first heard it. "Yeah, I had to listen to it a couple of times to get it. But I'm just glad you're still working." It was funny, but I thought, I'm just glad I'm still working.' It has multiple layers and many flavours, including soft rock, modern indie, funk and soul.

Of 'Cherry', he said: 'I wanted it to be true to the moment that I wrote it, and how I was feeling then [which was] not great,' he said. 'It's so pathetic in a way. The night that I wrote it, I was saying that I was feeling a lot of pressure because the last record wasn't a radio record. And I was like, "I feel like this record has to be really big. So I feel like I need to make certain songs."' So he stayed up all night and wrote 'Cherry'.

The song's genesis came when his engineer Sammy Witte was casually strumming an acoustic guitar riff one day. Harry happened to overhear, and loved it. It formed the starting point for the song's creation. Harry decided this was how he wanted his song to sound. The *Guardian* says this song sees Harry 'sing the blues'.

The French spoken words at the end came from a woman Harry was dating at the time. 'That's just a voice note of my ex-girlfriend talking,' he told *Rolling Stone*. 'I was playing guitar and she took a phone call – and she was actually speaking in the key of the song.' That woman is widely assumed to be the French model Camille Rowe.

On the track 'Falling', he said he wrote it in twenty minutes. He said that at that point he felt like he was 'becoming someone that I didn't want to be.' The dreamy track certainly helped portray and hopefully disperse that feeling.

Like with 'Cherry', it began when a member of his crew was casually playing an instrument. 'Tom had come up to my place to grab something, and he'd sat at the piano and I'd just got out of the shower,' said Harry. 'He started playing, and we wrote it there. So I was completely naked when I wrote that song.'

A nice image for the fans but it should not distract from what is a beautifully moving song. If you are going to cry during this album, this is likely to be the song that gets the tears rolling. That said, it was not to everyone's taste: the *NME* said the track was 'disappointing'.

For the next track, 'To Be So Lonely', the beginning of it all came when Harry himself was playing a guitalele – a ukulele with six strings. 'They're really good for writing on, because you can travel with them. I had one of those with me in Japan, so they're really good for spur-of-the-moment ideas,' he said. With its soaring violins and Spanish guitars, this is a rich tune, described as a sea shanty by some reviewers. The *Evening Standard* found this track and the one after it 'tedious'.

For those who were fans of the sprawling 'Sign of the Times', help is at hand in the next song – 'She'. Harry describes it as a 'phenomenal song'. He remembers how Mitch created the guitar part when he was 'a little, ah, influenced'.

Harry continues: 'Well, he was on mushrooms, we all were. We had no idea what we were doing. We forgot all about that track, then went back later and loved it. But Mitch had no idea what he did on guitar that night, so he had to learn it all over from the track.'

He says the song 'feels really British' and that to him it is definitely in the top three tracks on *Fine Line*. 'When I've been doing the track-listing, and ticking off the ones to definitely make the album, it's always in the first three to be ticked.'

Prince and Pink Floyd influences loom large on 'She'. Most of all, it confirms Harry as an artist of rock authenticity and a man of fine musical taste. Who could have guessed back in his days with One Direction that all this was bubbling away inside him? It is hard to imagine many former members of chart-topping boy bands producing a track like this and if, as the *Independent* felt, he indulged himself 'a little too much', it is not the worst thing.

'Sunflower, Vol. 6' sounds, says the *Guardian*, 'like it was bathed in southern California sunshine'. The *Independent* described it as a 'funky, syncopated psych-rock track'. The hand of the Beach Boys can be heard here, too, which *NOW* magazine indirectly acknowledged when it said it had 'beachside day drunk vibes'.

Joni Mitchell's influence can be felt deeply in 'Canyon Moon'. Harry had become so enthralled and obsessed with Joni Mitchell's 1971 classic *Blue* that he tracked down the woman who built the dulcimer Mitchell plays on that album. He got his first lesson in the instrument from the woman, Joellen Lapidus, at her house in Culver City. Harry says that the track that came from this is 'Crosby, Stills, and Nash on steroids'. 'I was in a pretty big Joni hole,' he says of the track.

> Harry had become so enthralled and obsessed with Joni Mitchell's 1971 classic *Blue* that he tracked down the woman who built the dulcimer Mitchell plays on that album.

On Harry's first solo tour, the slogan Treat People With Kindness was a constant. He told producer Jeff Bhasker one day that he would love to write a song with the slogan as the title. Jeff told him to go for it. 'It made me uncomfortable at first, because I wasn't sure what it was – but then I wanted to lean into that,' said Harry, adding that the upbeat tune 'opened something that's been in my core'. It couldn't be a happier or more uplifting tune and it certainly benefits from the presence of a Mellotron, the polyphonic style of keyboard first made famous by the Beatles. *Pitchfork* was not impressed, describing the song as 'an awful chimera of Jesus Christ Superstar'.

'Fine Line', the title track, closes the album. It is another one for fans of epic songs. It's also the most unorthodox tune, and this was no coincidence. 'It's a weird one,' Styles told *Rolling Stone*. 'It started simple, but I wanted to have this big epic outro thing. And it just took shape as this thing where I thought, "That's just like the music I want to make." I love strings, I love horns, I love harmonies – so why don't we just put all of that in there?'

Speaking to *Billboard,* he continued: 'The times when I felt good and I felt happy were the happiest I've ever felt in my life. And the times when I felt sad was the lowest I've ever felt in my life. And I think it was that feeling of when you can feel yourself falling back into one of those moments where you're there. The chorus says, "What am I now? Am I someone I don't want around?" It was a big moment where I was asking myself, "Who am I? What am I doing?"'

The *Guardian* said that when compared to his debut 'his idols – Bowie, Queen, Pink Floyd – are less to the fore as Styles begins to find his own niche,' adding that '*Fine Line* is a confident step in Styles's whimsical musical adventure'.

The *Independent* felt it was 'just a little too in thrall to music's greats' but added that while 'it may not reach the pinnacle of sex or sadness … *Fine Line* is a fine album nonetheless'.

The *NME* said the album is 'packed with personality and charm (and saucy lyrics)'. Hannah Mylrea added that 'for the most part … Styles's second album is a total joy. It's an elegant combination of the ex-boybander's influences, slick modern pop and his own roguish charm'.

Rolling Stone was delighted, saying: 'If there's a non-toxic masculinity, Harry Styles just might've found it.' *NOW* magazine said Harry 'finally sounds like he's living in his own time'.

The *Evening Standard* said *Fine Line* makes 'a strong argument for being the most interesting boy band escapee yet', adding that there was 'no crashingly obvious Sinatra covers or generic of-the-moment R&B'. David Smyth concludes: 'There's plenty he can be proud of here.'

The *New York Times* described the album's production as a 'tour de force' and lauded how 'Styles exults in sound, not image'.

Variety was somewhat more critical, saying 'sensuality and the melancholy are a little on the muted side, as if he weren't totally convinced he should be heartbroken over the break-up the record is supposed to be largely about'.

However, it added, while 'he's not necessarily ready to play the hero in a relationship yet, he's certainly coming off as one of the good guys in how he's defying blockbuster expectations by following his muse back into the classic rock era and casually claiming it as his own'.

The *Daily Telegraph* was also a tad underwhelmed, describing *Fine Line* as: 'charming but inconsequential'. The *Wall Street Journal's* boot can be felt going in as it describes *Fine Line* as 'more imitative than original' and providing 'no fresh perspective'.

Pitchfork lived up to its name when it said, 'Styles doesn't have the imagination of Bowie' and that his 'dullness is cast into sharp relief', with Jeremy D. Larson concluding: 'mostly I hear a guy who's still afraid he'll never make a David Bowie record'.

Consequences of Sound said: '*Fine Line* is often disarmingly vulnerable and brimming with cunning observations, yet it's also woefully short on moments of unadulterated rawk, content to smoulder when a fireball of sexual bravado would have been preferred.'

His former bandmate Liam Payne has previously been critical of

Harry's solo music, as we have seen. But after hearing album two, Liam was more impressed and was trying to hitch himself onto the Harry Styles bandwagon. 'From the first song off his album, I feel like me and Harry could do a really cool song together,' he said on the Hits Radio Breakfast Show, speaking of *Fine Line* and the first single from it, 'Lights Up'.

'There could be a good mix between the two things because the first song was kind of funky so I feel like we could break down into some sort of hip-hop-R&B thing halfway through, and have like a little megamix,' Payne explained.

Later, Liam spoke of his distant relationship with Harry. He began his remarks with a reference to his healthy relationships with Louis and Niall. 'But with Harry, there's so much mystery around who he's become. I was looking at some pictures of him the other day, and I just thought: "I don't know what more I'd say to him other than, 'Hello' and 'How are you?'"' I mean, look at the stuff I put out and the stuff Harry puts out. Polar opposite,' he added, referencing Styles's soft-rock music and his own hip-hop-oriented work. 'I'm like the Antichrist version of what Harry is.'

* * *

Indeed, it felt for a while that every time Liam popped up in an interview he would mention Harry. Speaking to *GQ* in 2019, he said: 'Now the band members have all worked our way through this first couple of years, you can kind of see everyone's finding their own feet. Take Harry at the moment. You know, he's just found what I think is his sound and exactly where he wants to be, which took him a little minute to get into since he had his last album out.'

That same year, he reunited with Harry after not having seen him for a long time. 'We spoke about a number of things, we hadn't seen each other for three years. Literally I hadn't seen him once, we hadn't spoken or anything. He was pretty much the same boy that I left him. We spoke about kids and happiness and all sorts of stuff,' he said on *Watch What Happens Live with Andy Cohen*.

Harry was assured enough to believe in his album with or without the approval of Payne. 'I wanted to see if I could write something that people liked, without knowing everything about me,' he told a documentary. In that case, his album was definitely a success. Asked about whether individuals had influenced the songs directly, he told the *Guardian*: 'If a song's about someone, is that fine? Or is that gonna get annoying for them, if people try to decipher it?'

It might have been a case of once-bitten-twice-shy for Harry after his experiences around his debut. 'I look back on the last album and I thought I was being so honest, just because there's one line about having a wank,' he told *Rolling Stone*.

'I had no idea. You write a song that's pretty open and honest, and you think, "That's just my song," but then you hand it over to people, and it's like, "Oh fuck!" Until people hear them, they're not even songs. They're just voice notes.'

'There are up tracks, down tracks, some with the trippy delirium of harpsichord-era Stones, others with the angsty Britpop swell of strings.'

Voice notes that became wonderful songs that made up an astonishing album. Tom Lamont of the *Guardian* was one of the writers to notice just what a leap Harry had made since his days of 'What Makes You Beautiful' with One Direction. 'The new album, *Fine Line*, is at its best when capturing late-hours moments, drunk calls, "wandering hands", kitchen snogs,' Lamont wrote. 'A golden-haired lover recurs. There are up tracks, down tracks, some with the trippy delirium of harpsichord-era Stones, others with the angsty Britpop swell of strings.'

However, Harry's new path should not be taken to read that he disliked the direction he took with the band that made him famous. 'I know it's the thing that always happens. When somebody gets out of a band, they go, "That wasn't me. I was held back." But it was me,' he told *Rolling Stone*. 'And I don't feel like I was held back at all. It was so much fun. If I didn't enjoy it, I wouldn't have done it. It's not like I was tied to a radiator.'

The final word on the album should go to Harry's close friend Tom Hull, who gave the singer this advice when he was setting out on the new work. 'Just date amazing women, or men, or whatever, who are going to fuck you up … Let it affect you and write songs about it,' he said.

Well, that's one way of getting yourself inspired.

CHAPTER TWELVE

IN PUBLIC AND
PRIVATE

As we have seen, just as fame can bring huge riches to those lucky enough to reach pop music's top tier, it also comes with a price. Harry faced the negative side when a homeless man locked on to him and was convicted of stalking him. After being freaked out by the man, who had behaved increasingly oddly around him, Harry felt he had no option but to take a legal route to resolve the problem.

In the autumn of 2019, the case went to Hendon Magistrates' Court in north London. Here, Harry spoke from behind a screen, giving testimony to the court about his uncomfortable experiences, telling the story of how it all unfolded.

During a testing court hearing, Harry had said he was left feeling 'scared' and 'very uncomfortable' by the behaviour of twenty-six-year-old Pablo Tarazaga-Orero, who had posted notes and money through his letter box. The defendant had also camped outside Harry's house and, according to the singer, 'lunged' at him when he was out running.

The singer told the court that the saga had begun when he offered Tarazaga-Orero money for food or a hotel after noticing him sleeping rough near his north London home. 'I thought it was sad that someone so young was sleeping rough at a bus stop when it was cold,' he testified.

In response to the offer of food, Tarazaga-Orero, a vegan, asked for edamame beans, the court heard. Harry said he felt this was an odd request. The following day, the singer returned with two sandwiches, two salads and two muffins from a vegan cafe but quickly decided to stop interacting with the defendant because of his increasingly 'odd' behaviour that made Harry feel 'a little uneasy'.

However, despite Harry's decision to cut all contact, this was not the end of the story. Styles said he would still see Tarazaga-Orero 'incredibly often … almost every day', and he was followed by the defendant, who posted coins to the value of £49.50 through his door. Harry also said he was followed into a local pub a number of times and stopped on a jog by Tarazaga-Orero, who asked for money. He told the court his stalker had 'lunged' at him and 'blocked his path' as he went running one evening.

Individually the examples might seem just a little disturbing, but when taken together, it's easy to imagine why Harry began to feel very freaked out by it all. He explained he was still affected by the other man's actions, so had 'employed a night guard' and continued 'to lock my bedroom door at night'.

Others gave evidence in the case, adding to the uncomfortable account. For instance, Harry's neighbour, Rafal Krzeszewski, told the court he spoke to Tarazaga-Orero after he started camping at a bus stop near Harry's home. The delivery driver said: 'He said he is a soulmate of my neighbour, Harry Styles, and he's in love.'

Tarazaga-Orero, who was arrested after he returned from his native Spain, also gave evidence. He denied the charge, telling Hendon Magistrates' Court the star had in fact propositioned him. After swearing on the *Bhagavad Gita* holy book, the defendant testified that he chose to sleep in north London as it felt safer than the West End and he never intended to stalk the singer, but 'just wanted the money he offered me'.

He also said Harry propositioned him and alleged he was told: '"Let's come to a hotel, let's have some fun", or something like that.' In a particularly testing moment, Harry had been forced to deny this claim. He replied: 'I did not' after defence barrister Jenni Dempster QC asked: 'Did you suggest both of you could have gone to a hotel to have fun?'

Ultimately, Tarazaga-Orero was disbelieved and banned from going within 250 metres of the singer. He was also banned from posting online about Harry, made the subject of a twelve-month community order and told to complete a thirty-day rehabilitation requirement.

Giving his verdict and reasons, District Judge Nigel Dean said: 'It would be fair for me to say at this stage that I found Mr Styles to be a reliable and credible witness. It seemed to me that he was doing his best to assist the court. I didn't find any major inconsistencies or shortcomings in relation to his evidence.

'Mr Styles felt sorry for a young man who he saw to be living without a home during the winter when it was cold and raining very heavily and having first noticed him he then out of the goodness of his heart stopped and offered to fund the defendant's hotel accommodation that evening.

'I found the suggestion that he would accompany the defendant for fun to be completely incredible. These were honest, well intended, good intentions from somebody who was trying to help another for whom he felt sorry and who he thought was down on his luck.

'He knew perfectly well that what he was doing at that stage amounted to harassment of Mr Styles. I'm quite satisfied that this behaviour had the effect of harassing Mr Styles.'

Speaking directly to the defendant, the judge said: 'You should be aware that failing to comply with a community order is a criminal offence and carries a maximum five-year prison sentence.'

Although Harry was relieved at the verdict, there was an understanding that the story had to be handled delicately from a public relations perspective. For Harry, one of the planet's richest celebrities, to be in court against a homeless man could be mishandled by mischievous elements of the media. So a prepared statement was read out reflecting Harry's position. Prosecutor Katy Weiss told the court she had spoken to Harry on Sunday and he was 'adamant he wants [the defendant] to get help, although he doesn't want to see him again'.

Many famous people have had problems with stalkers. Pop legend Justin Timberlake took a restraining order out against a forty-eight-year-old fan who was caught loitering on his Hollywood estate for the third time. For some members of the public such excitable fans can seem essentially harmless. Perhaps, they argue, this is just a by-product of fame that celebs should get used to? But Harry's fellow *X Factor* alumnus Leona Lewis could offer a very different perspective. A twenty-nine-year-old man once queued at a Waterstones bookshop for a reported five hours to see Lewis, who was promoting her book, then, when he finally reached the front, punched her in the face. He was arrested at the scene.

In 2018, Michael Shawn Hunt was convicted of stalking the singer Lana Del Rey. The forty-three-year-old was arrested with a knife outside Del Rey's concert in Orlando. He was sentenced to one year in prison after agreeing to a plea deal in which he pleaded no contest to a stalking charge.

While there is no suggestion at all that Tarazaga-Orero had

any such behaviour planned, these stories give an insight into why celebrities are extremely sensitive about stalkers, and why Harry felt the need to get a bodyguard.

He had another unpleasant experience with crime in 2020, when he was mugged at knifepoint in London on Valentine's Day. According to *Mirror Online*, he was on a night out when he was confronted by a man who pulled out a knife and demanded cash. Harry quickly handed over the cash, and was left unharmed.

Police confirmed that 'officers were contacted on Saturday 15 February regarding the incident which happened at 23.50hrs on Friday 14 February'. They added: 'It was reported that a man in his 20s was approached by another man and threatened him with a knife. The victim was not injured, however, cash was taken from him. No arrests and enquiries are ongoing.'

A source said: 'He actually played it pretty cool, quickly giving the assailant cash, keeping himself and the guy calm and getting the situation over with. Understandably, though, it left him very shaken up afterwards.' With the news of Caroline Flack's death coming within hours of the mugging, it turned into a testing weekend for Harry. However, he put on a brave face on the BRIT Awards red carpet days later, looking sharp in a double-breasted purple pant suit with a lace-collared pale blue shirt and violet wool sweater underneath. Yet even at the BRIT Awards, he faced irritation when he was accused of being 'insensitive' to Storm Dennis flood victims by using a water feature in his performance. What a few days he had had.

★ ★ ★

As two singers with a cheeky sense of humour who found fame in their teens, Harry and Adele have plenty in common. In January 2020, the two singers made regular headlines when they holidayed together in the Caribbean, with Harry's friend James Corden along with them. Photos of Harry wearing a Mickey Mouse T-shirt during their break were overshadowed by the photographs of Adele showing a dramatic weight loss during their vacation, on the glamorous island of Anguilla. There was also plenty of press excitement when they left a huge £1,545 tip after dining together at a restaurant at New Year.

The trip marked quite a moment for the pair, as they have some history. Nine years earlier, when Harry was just seventeen years old, he said in an interview with Capital FM that he had a crush on Adele and that she made him 'weak at the knees'. When she described him as 'cute' in another interview, he spoke about her again, saying he would love to date the 'incredible' singer.

The following year, during the BRIT Awards, Harry told the *Mirror* that he would 'definitely' like to kiss Adele. When asked by the paper which stars he would like to kiss during the awards party, he said: 'Adele, definitely Adele.' Soon, they were in touch. Appearing on Radio 1, after he had turned twenty-one, he said: 'For my twenty-first she gave me one of her albums, *21*, and said, "I did some pretty cool stuff when I was twenty-one, good luck." I was like, "Geez."'

The first confirmed meeting between the two came in 2016, when Harry was working on his single 'Sign of the Times'. He said: 'I've spoken to her a little bit, she knows one of the guys that I wrote [his album] with a lot.' But when they actually holidayed together, the rumour mill went into overdrive. According to some, Harry was Adele's 'rock' following her split from husband Simon Konecki. A source told *Closer*: 'Harry was Adele's rock when she split from Simon last April. He checked in on her constantly, stayed over at her LA mansion whenever she needed company, and generally was an amazing friend to her when she most needed it.'

They added: 'Harry's always been very health-conscious. After Adele vowed to get in shape, he said he wanted to help her, so took her hiking on some of his favourite trails in Malibu, occasionally did

HIIT classes with her, and gave her a hand with meal-planning and cooking to help her stay on track.' It was also claimed that Harry had introduced Adele to Bulletproof coffee – a black coffee drink mixed with butter and coconut oil that he reportedly uses to curb his appetite.

Meanwhile, said the source, Adele was starting to fall for Harry. 'While they've always been flirtatious, she says it's only in the last month that she's started to see him in a romantic light,' they were quoted as saying. 'It's still early days, but she hasn't ruled out exploring their chemistry and connection. She's finally back to her best and feels ready to explore a relationship with a new man, whether that's with Harry or someone else.'

> While they've always been flirtatious, she says it's only in the last month that she's started to see him in a romantic light.

How realistic this speculation is remains to be confirmed. Would the two be compatible as lovers? What is clear is that they have things in common as artists and stars. This is particularly true in terms of their attitudes to exposure – where both are willing to disappear from the public eye in a way that is quite old-fashioned in these days of celebrities tirelessly reminding us of their existence.

Adele had a prolonged absence between the release of 21 and its follow-up 25, four years later. A good insight into the poise of that absence is made clear by comparing what her fellow female superstars did during the same time. Taylor Swift released two albums (Red and 1989) and tried to become a spokeswoman for a generation; Lady Gaga offered two (Born This Way and Artpop), while Katy Perry released just the one (Prism).

However, it is not only in the number of releases that we see how Adele stood out. It is in the absence of ancillary aspects of celebrity that we see how she differs. During that four-year hiatus between albums, she essentially disappeared. No interviews, public appearances or cynically engineered publicity stunts were fixed to keep her profile up.

This old-fashioned approach to fame, with mystique where others might have desperation, gave Adele the image more of an icon than a celebrity – a term that has become sullied in the twenty-first century. Harry, too, has some of what Adele has. For the public to install a singer as an icon, and to take that icon to their hearts, there must be two, seemingly paradoxical, things about them: knowledge and mystery. In other words, the public must feel like they both know the artist well and do not know them at all.

It is quite a skill to maintain that balance but Harry is treading the tightrope well. For a long time, we all felt like we knew Harry. He was the guy who popped up one Saturday night as we sat watching *The X Factor*. We thought he was cute but also a bit cocky, in an inoffensive way. Right from the start he clearly had some of that dust that makes someone special, yet we watched as he turned from a cheeky boy into a global star.

✶ ✶ ✶

From the moment he announced himself to the universe with a cheeky grin at his first *X Factor* audition in 2010, Harry has ridden the rollercoaster of fame with aplomb. Even during the dips in that ride, he has yet to face the sort of fully-formed backlash that many celebrities endure these days, but, in 2022, he got his first hint of how that might feel, as he was forced to weather a storm of controversy, the likes of which he'd never encountered before.

He was cast in *Don't Worry Darling*, an American psychological thriller directed by Olivia Wilde, which follows the fortunes of a housewife living an idyllic life in an experimental company town who begins to suspect a sinister secret is being kept from its residents by the man who runs it.

Styles was a late addition to the cast after Shia LaBeouf left the production. In an Instagram post that described his 'humility and grace', Wilde gushed with gratitude over Harry's attitude during filming. There was plenty to be gracious about behind the scenes, if the rumour mill were to be believed. It was reported that actress Florence Pugh had a feud with Wilde and declined to take a full role in promotion. Then Wilde claimed she had fired Shia LaBeouf from the cast due to a 'no asshole policy' but then LaBeouf released a video of Wilde pleading with him to return to the movie. Clearly all was far from well.

When the movie was released, the critics were very unkind. The *Guardian's* Peter Bradshaw gave the film two stars, describing it as an 'unconvincing tale of dystopian suburbia' and the *Daily Mail* gave it the same score, with reviewer Brian Viner describing Harry's performance as a 'trifle mechanical'. Anthony Lane of the *New Yorker* described Styles as 'utterly and helplessly adrift'.

BBC Culture's Steph Green said he 'doesn't feel up to the material here, with leaden line delivery and a lack of light and shade making his scenes opposite Pugh fall flat', while the *Independent's* Geoffrey Macnab described him as 'charisma-free'. This was the closest Harry had come to a critical kicking and might have made him doubt the wisdom of his late decision to join the cast in the first place.

An aspect of Harry's performance in the movie that boggled a lot of minds was his accent. As soon as a preview clip featuring him emerged online in August 2022, the sneak peek left many viewers asking what accent he was attempting and whether his character was British or American. 'Why is Harry Styles, allegedly English, doing such a bad English accent?' wondered one cynic on Twitter, while another quipped:

What is the accent Harry Styles is aiming for in *Don't Worry Darling*? I need to know before I can sleep again.

'What is the accent Harry Styles is aiming for in *Don't Worry Darling*? I need to know before I can sleep again.'

Harry might have felt some renewed kinship with his former band-mate Liam Payne. During a live TV interview at the Oscars, many viewers were baffled by Payne's accent, describing it as everything from American, to Irish and Dutch. Asked later about his meandering enunciation, Payne said that he was a 'social chameleon' who picked up the accents of people he spent time with. Harry, meanwhile, said he understood Payne's varied voice, saying of his own accent that 'it's a little bit all over the place because I'm from up North and lived in London for ten years, and spent a lot of time in America and stuff'.

For all the discord among cast and crew, there was also some romance: the rumour mill suggested that Harry was spending a lot of time with the film's director, Wilde, who was ten years his senior. However, in November 2022, it was revealed that she and Harry had decided to take a 'break' after nearly two years of dating. 'Harry didn't dump Olivia, or vice versa,' an insider told *Page Six*. 'It's impossible to have a relationship when he's in every continent next year and Olivia has her job and her kids.'

For someone whose musical efforts were so immediately and dramatically praised, Harry was discovering that his acting would not be such an instant hit. His next movie, *My Policeman*, also attracted criticism and conjured controversy for him. The story of a 1950s forbidden love triangle, the project was ripe for a row from the start. During an interview with *Rolling Stone*, he was challenged on whether he was 'queerbaiting', or profiting from taking on 'queer aesthetics' without identifying himself as a member of the queer community.

His answer seemingly dismissed the concern. 'Some people say, "you've only publicly been with women," and I don't think I've publicly been with anyone,' he said. 'If someone takes a picture of you with someone, it doesn't mean you're choosing to have a public relationship or something.' He also caused offence when he said the movie would portray gay sex as 'tender and loving' and claimed that 'so much of gay sex in film is two guys going at it, and it kind of removes the tenderness from it'. Although these words were seemingly supportive of the gay community, the suggestion that cinema suffers from an abundance of 'two guys going at it' caused anger, said *Dazed*, because the claim 'doesn't bear any scrutiny whatsoever'.

There were tough verdicts over his performance in general. The *Hollywood Reporter* said 'he's not terrible, but he leaves a hole in the movie where a more multidimensional character with an inner life is needed most' and *Variety* said that 'you ache for him every time a bit of dialogue thuds'. While the *Los Angeles Times* was more admiring, saying 'Styles carries the day', another harsh verdict was not far behind, with the *Washington Post* describing him as 'flat'.

However, all this negativity was a mere pinprick compared to the fuller flesh wound he suffered when it was speculated that he had spat at his *Don't Worry Darling* co-star, Chris Pine, during the movie's premiere in Venice. It was hoped that the rumoured behind-the-scenes chaos could be brushed aside, or at least under the carpet, however, the instantly infamous 'SpitGate' clip from the evening put paid to that.

The *Guardian* said the footage of the alleged spit was 'one of the most bizarre clips that has ever made it to the internet'. The clip begins as stars are arriving in their seats for the premiere. Chris Pine is seen sitting somewhat awkwardly in his seat, with Wilde on one side and an empty chair on the other. When Harry appears in the frame, he has one collar sticking out of his blue suit. As he reaches the seats, he pauses, briefly glances at Pine's lap and then sits down. Pine stops applauding suddenly and looks down at his own lap, shaking his head in shock. Immediately, it was speculated that he was shocked because Harry had spat into his lap.

Those commenting on the internet quickly fell into one of three camps: some said Harry had spat in disdain, some said he had spat as an agreed prank between the pair, and some said there had been no spit at all.

Soon, supporting evidence for the 'spit' theory was presented in the form of a clip of Harry and Pine during a promotional interview. According to the 'spit lobby', this showed that all was not well between the pair. 'You know, my favourite thing about the movie is it feels like a movie,' Harry says, as his co-star appears to stare off into the distance, with quiet disdain. 'It feels like a real go-to-the-theatre film, movie, that you know … the reason why you go, to watch something on the big screen.'

However, Pine's team issued a denial of the spit theory. 'Just to be clear, Harry Styles did not spit on Chris Pine,' they told *People*, adding that 'there is nothing but respect between these two men and any suggestion otherwise is a blatant attempt to create drama that simply does not exist'. Harry addressed the controversy in the form of a quip during a concert at Madison Square Garden. 'Wonderful to be back in New York! I just popped very quickly to Venice to spit on Chris Pine,' he joked, before giggling at the absurdity of the episode.

* * *

Although the road to movie stardom may be proving rocky, Harry's music is going from strength to strength. His third album was a success critically and commercially, winning him Album of the Year at the 2023 Grammys – unequivocally the biggest prize at the prestigious event. It was clearly the album that reflected him best. The imprint of the man on the work was evident right from its title: *Harry's House*. The tracks took fans and casual listeners alike into his realm – and people liked what they found there.

'Music for a Sushi Restaurant' was inspired when Harry was in a sushi restaurant in Los Angeles with his producer and the track 'Watermelon Sugar' came over the speakers. He said he thought it was 'really strange music for a sushi restaurant'. The R&B vibe of 'Late Night Talking' is another track to put a spring in the step of the listener and takes the happy vibe of the album to a new level.

The Paul McCartney feel of 'Grapejuice' has drawn comparisons with The Beatles but the chorus is the closest he has come to a One Direction sound for a while. However, track four sees the attention return back to Harry himself. 'As It Was' is an 'effervescent, high-tempo hit to have you clicking your heels', said the *Guardian*, while *Rolling Stone* felt it was an 'irresistible dance-floor challenge'. While the vocals are self-referential and vulnerable at times, the synth-pop keeps the song on a high.

Other standout tracks include 'Matilda', where Harry channels his heroine Joni Mitchell to render a moving ode to an unloved child struggling amid the challenges and confusion of the modern world. It was inspired by a relationship he had with someone experiencing such difficulty. 'Sometimes it's just about listening,' he told interviewer Zane Lowe. 'I hope that's what I did here. If nothing else, it just says, "I was listening to you".' 'Keep Driving', with its imagery of Los Angeles, and 'Satellite' with its powerful climax, both take the album close to the highs of its strong opening. 'Boyfriends', another notable track, is about difficult relationships and is perhaps the smoothest he has ever sounded.

The album 'ticks a lot of the right boxes and has abundant charm, which makes it a perfect reflection of the pop star who made it', said the *Guardian*. It is 'undoubtedly Styles' best record yet', felt *NME*, and 'presents a musician comfortable and confident in what he wants to create right now'. The *Independent* said he navigates 'grief and regret with a funk soul panache' and *Entertainment Weekly* said the collection 'gently nudges the expectations of what pop should sound like'. As for Harry himself, he has described this record as his 'biggest and the most fun, but by far the most intimate'.

It was also a smash-hit around the world. Just two hours after *Harry's House* was released on Apple Music, it earned the most first-day streams for a pop album released in 2022. It debuted at number one in the UK and US, and ultimately topped the charts in twenty-eight other countries, too, from Hungary to Argentina.

He could hardly wait to take the album on the road. His concert tour, named 'Love On Tour', was disrupted by the Covid pandemic and therefore has straddled two album releases: *Fine Line* and *Harry's House*. 'Yes, he dispenses charisma like a fire hose; no, he couldn't be sexier if he tried,' said the *Los Angeles Times*; while on the east coast, *The New York Times* praised his 'off-the-charts charisma' and 'collective exuberance'. In the UK, *Metro* said his performance was a 'spellbinding and electric experience packed with joy and heart' and the *Guardian* said he was 'admirably sure-footed'.

Meanwhile, Harry shows no sign of resting on his laurels. He is too ambitious and restless an artist for that. As 2022 drew to a close and he looked back on a year of highs and lows, he was reminded of his inspirations when he learned that one of his musical heroes, the Fleetwood Mac singer Christine McVie, had died after a short illness.

He paid tribute to her during a show in Chile, performing 'Songbird', a tender piano ballad, written and performed by McVie, from the band's album *Rumours*. At the end of his performance, Harry said: 'Thank you, Christine,' and blew a kiss to the sky.

WHAT WILL BECOME OF HARRY?

His place in the pop music world is currently secure, but what might become of Harry Styles in this fickle industry? Robbie Williams remains the UK standard-bearer for a successful member of a boy band who has gone on to make a success of himself as a solo act. He is as good a benchmark to measure against as any.

Like One Direction, his band, Take That, became a massive success. After their formation in 1989, they became imperious in the pop world. In total, they enjoyed no fewer than twenty-eight top 40 singles and seventeen top 5 singles in the UK Singles Chart, twelve of which were number ones, including the anthemic 'Back for Good' and 'Never Forget'. They have also had eight number-one albums on the UK Albums Chart. On the international stage, the band have had fifty-six number-one singles and thirty-nine number-one albums.

Williams left the band early, quitting in 1995. As the remaining members continued for another twelve months, he embarked on a solo career that would, in many ways, outstrip even the success of the band. As of the end of 2022, he could boast seven UK number-one singles, and eleven out of his twelve studio albums have reached number one in the UK. He is the best-selling British solo artist in the United Kingdom; no fewer than six of his albums are among the top 100 biggest-selling albums ever in the UK. He is also a record-breaker: in 2006 he entered the *Guinness Book of World Records* for selling 1.6 million tickets for his 'Close Encounters' tour in a single day.

However, alongside this success has been a well-documented struggle with mental health, involving addictions, fluctuating weight, personal demons and other challenges. How much these issues are a result of his fame, and whether he would have suffered just as much without the glare of the spotlight, is up for discussion.

But certainly from a pop-career point of view, he has set an example of a path to try to follow and a path to try to avoid. Who would not wish for his level of success? Who would want any of the issues that ran alongside it? There seemed a rich symbolism for Harry in particular when it was Williams who was chosen to be One Direction's duet during the *X Factor* final. In the pre-song VT, Harry said: 'I think that is incredible – that he'd even consider doing a duet with us.'

And yet, during the performance itself, Harry stood out as remarkably at ease with the whole concept. As Liam, Louis, Niall and Zayn looked like little boys who had won some sort of charity prize to sing with their hero, Harry stood with more assurance. No wide eyes from Harry, just insouciance and charisma. Much like the man they were singing with, in fact.

Harry has noted what addiction has done to people, as he revealed in *i-D* magazine. He spoke compassionately of the topic but also, thankfully, with a distance. 'We all know addiction is an illness that affects so many people,' he said, adding that it is 'still cloaked in so much secrecy and shame'. While there are no signs yet of Harry developing any of the emotional issues that plagued Williams, those in his team would be very happy if he could match his commercial success. Yet they can already perhaps point to ways that Harry has arguably surpassed Williams' success. His success and fame in the USA are things that Williams sweated buckets for years to try to achieve. Then there is the level of individuality Harry has found. It is difficult to imagine much of his solo material appearing anywhere near a One Direction album. Yet Williams' solo songs, magnificent as many of them were, hardly broke away from the sort of material Take That were busy with. In fact, Williams' attempts to rebel away from the path of his former band often felt desperate, whereas Harry has sashayed away. Where Williams released the widely panned *Rudebox* and tried to engineer himself into the affections of Mancunian rockers Oasis, only to be mocked by the Gallaghers as 'that fat dancer from Take That', Harry has achieved credibility more effortlessly.

Indeed, since One Direction went their separate ways, Harry has managed to build a shroud of mystery around himself, even as he became the most famous former member of that juggernaut pop band. In *i-D* magazine, he said that keeping this balance was 'something I learned over time'. He explained: 'Especially starting out, because when you first start, you're encouraged to give as much as you can. But it goes back to separating work from the rest of your life. Realizing that there are things that you need to keep to yourself and things that you don't have to share with anyone. It keeps everything a little nicer.' As such, he is setting an example; *Esquire* noted this when they declared that Harry's 'flagrant rule breaking is now the new rulebook'.

* * *

In these days of divisive politics, populism and global upheaval, Harry has hinted that his material might become more political in the future. In *i-D* magazine, he said: 'We're living in a time where it's impossible not to be aware of what's going on in the world. Society has never been so divisive. It's important to stand up for what we think is right. I would love for my views to come through in the music I make and the things I do. That's a very powerful way that we can use our voices. I think for a long time people thought "what I do doesn't matter" but revolution comes from small acts, and now people are realizing that's what sparks real change.'

The positive reception for *Fine Line* and *Harry's House* were, clearly, very convenient for Harry's future. Sometimes former boy-band members are mocked if they try to position themselves as serious solo artists. The media and public refuse to accept that anyone who has been in a pop band could ever mature into a more serious act. You can only be one or the other, they insist.

Looking to the future, Harry is keeping his cards close to his chest regarding the big question on a lot of lips: the prospect of a One Direction reunion. 'I don't know,' he said when *Rolling Stone* asked him about the chances of it. 'I don't think I'd ever say I'd never do it again, because I don't feel that way. If there's a time when we all really want to do it, that's the only time for us to do it, because I don't think it should be about anything else other than the fact that we're all like, "Hey, this was really fun. We should do this again." But until that time, I feel like I'm really enjoying making music and experimenting. I enjoy making music this way too much to see myself doing a full switch, to go back and do that again. Because I also think if we went back to doing things the same way, it wouldn't be the same, anyway.'

He added: 'Above all else, we're the people who went through that. We're always going to have that, even if we're not the closest. And the fact is, just because you're in a band with someone doesn't mean you have to be best friends. That's not always how it works. Just because Fleetwood Mac fight, that doesn't mean they're not amazing. I think even in the disagreements, there's always a mutual respect for each other – we did this really cool thing together, and we'll always have that. It's too important to me to ever be like, "Oh, that's done." But if it happens it will happen for the right reasons.'

The other former members of One Direction have varied opinions on the prospect of the band getting back together. Louis Tomlinson, for instance, has spoken of being fairly desperate for such a reunion. Harry remains cool and collected about it. It would be easy to simply credit his self-assurance to the fame and fortune he has acquired over the past ten years. But the roots of it go much further back than that, all the way to 1994 and his mother Anne, who brought him up beautifully and thoughtfully. Many stars seek the spotlight to grab some of the love and attention they lacked as children in the family home.

For Harry, he had a loving and attentive mother. A childhood home that echoed with laughter. Anne backed him when he chased fame but never pushed him into it. She loves him the same as an international superstar as she did when he worked in a bakery. Since the days of One Direction, Harry has not lacked fans. But in his mother he has the best champion anyone could ask for.

At twenty-nine years of age, Harry has achieved an awful lot, including five albums with a band, three solo albums, parts in four movies and various commercial deals. By twenty-nine, many pop stars have faded away entirely, or are on a clear downward trajectory, with their best years behind them. Yet, with Harry, the sense that the best is yet to come is inescapable. There will be more chapters in this remarkable life.

DISCOGRAPHY

ONE DIRECTION

SINGLES

What Makes You Beautiful (2011)

Gotta Be You (2011)

One Thing (2012)

More Than This (2012)

Live While We're Young (2012)

Little Things (2012)

Kiss You (2013)

One Way Or Another (Teenage Kicks)
(2013)

Best Song Ever (2013)

Story of My Life (2013)

Midnight Memories (2014)

You & I (2014)

Steal My Girl (2014)

Night Changes (2014)

Drag Me Down (2015)

Perfect (2015)

History (2015)

ALBUMS

Up All Night (2011)

Take Me Home (2012)

Midnight Memories (2013)

Four (2014)

Made in the A.M. (2015)

SOLO

SINGLES

Sign of the Times (2017)

Two Ghosts (2017)

Kiwi (2017)

Lights Up (2019)

Watermelon Sugar (2019)

Adore You (2019)

Falling (2020)

Watermelon Sugar (2020)

Golden (2020)

Treat People With Kindness (2021)

Fine Line (2021)

As It Was (2022)

Late Night Talking (2022)

Music For A Sushi Restaurant (2022)

ALBUMS

Harry Styles (2017)

Fine Line (2019)

Harry's House (2022)

FILMOGRAPHY

Dunkirk (2017)

Eternals (2021)

Don't Worry Darling (2022)

My Policeman (2022)

ACKNOWLEDGEMENTS

Working on this book as the world changed around us has been therapeutic. So thank you to Louise Dixon, Gabby Nemeth and the rest of the wonderful team at Michael O'Mara Books.

Huge thanks also to everyone who has supported and encouraged my writing over the years, especially Lucian and Chris. Thanks also to Harry (not that one) for the cuddles.

BIBLIOGRAPHY

Adele: The Biography, Chas Newkey-Burden, John Blake, 2015

Birth Order: What Your Position in the Family Really Tells You about Your Character, Linda Blair, Piatkus, 2013

Harry Styles: The Biography, Offstage, Ali Cronin, Penguin, 2017

Harry Styles: Every Piece of Me, Louisa Jepson, Simon & Schuster, 2013

Harry Styles: Evolution of a Modern Superstar, Malcolm Croft, Carlton, 2018

One Direction: Dare to Dream, Harper Collins, 2011

1D – The One Direction Story: An Unauthorized Biography, Danny White, Michael O'Mara, 2012

Taylor Swift: The Whole Story, Chas Newkey-Burden, Harper Collins, 2014

The Artist's Way, Julia Cameron, Macmillan, 1994

PICTURE CREDITS

Page 1: McPix Ltd / Shutterstock (top); Richard Young / Shutterstock (bottom)

Page 2: EDB Image Archive / Alamy

Page 3: Ian Gavan / Getty Images (top); Fred Duval / FilmMagic / Getty Images (bottom)

Page 4: David Fisher / Shutterstock (top); © Motoo Naka / AFLO / Alamy (bottom)

Page 5: WENN Rights Ltd / Alamy (top); David Fisher / Shutterstock (bottom)

Page 6: Jon Furniss / Invision / AP / Shutterstock (top); Startraks / Shutterstock (bottom)

Page 7: Bret Hartman / CBS via Getty Images (top); Gustavo Caballero / Getty Images (bottom)

Page 8: Jon Kopaloff / FilmMagic / Getty Images

Page 9: Mark Robert Milan / Getty Images

Page 10: Beretta / Sims / Shutterstock (top); Warner Bros / Kobal / Shutterstock (bottom)

Page 11: Tristan Fewings / Getty Images (top); Eamonn M. McCormack / WPA Pool / Getty Images (bottom)

Page 12: John Angelillo / UPI / Getty Images (top); J. Kempin / Getty Images for NBC (bottom)

Page 13: Terence Patrick / CBS via Getty Images (top); Rich Fury / Getty Images for Spotify (bottom)

Page 14: Roma / IPA Milestone Media / PA Images (top); Matt Winkelmeyer / MG19 / Getty Images for The Met Museum / Vogue (bottom)

Page 15: JM Enternational / Shutterstock (top); JM Enternational / JM Enternational for Brit Awards / Getty Images (bottom)

Page 16: Joseph Okpako / WireImage / Getty Images (top); Franco Origlia / Getty Images (bottom)

INDEX